T0149145

R E A L
CARDIFF

rhiwbina

whitchurch

river rumney

cyncoed

heath

st fagans

llandaff

roath

plasnewydd

lambies

riverside

splott

adamsdown

canton

newtown

ely

central

river taff

grangetown

butetown

river ely

the
bay

bristol
channel

the city

flat holm

REAL
CARDIFF

PETER FINCH

SEREN

Seren is the book imprint of
Poetry Wales Press Ltd
Nolton Street, Bridgend, Wales
www.seren-books.com

ISBN 1-85411-385-2

A CIP record for this title is available from
the British Library

The publisher works with the financial assistance
of the Welsh Books Council

Printed by Bell & Bain Ltd, Glasgow

Some earlier versions of parts of this book have appeared
in various numbers of *Planet*, as well as in the British Council's
book of cross cultural writing from the UK, *Identity Papers*.
A number of the poems appeared in *Poetry Salzburg Review*.
Larger sections appeared on the web as part of the
Peter Finch Archive at *www.peterfinch.co.uk*

For Dan, Will and Belinda

CONTENTS

PREFACE

Cities are the most post-modern of devices in the way they mix, re-write and over-write their histories. The present is only as real as the past which gets dubbed onto it. Could the city of this book still be Cardiff?

What began as a commission to write a piece about the dramatic changes taking place in the capital of Wales during the late 1990s has turned into a total obsession. I have John Barnie, editor of *Planet*, to thank for that. Take a walk around, he asked me, write down what you see. You were born there. Explain Cardiff to us. The proposition has proved far more engaging than I'd imagined.

Yes, I am a Cardiff native, one who still lives in the city too. And in the circles in which I move there are not many of us about. But that didn't mean at the time of the commission that I *knew* the city: deeply, intrinsically, like the palm of my hand. What I knew were parts, slices, rumours, tales, fragments. To write the article (and the book which followed) I needed to study the history, check the context, investigate the loose ends, and revisit, go back to the bits I thought I knew and look again. At first I took on the role of sponge – buying up everything I could find with 'Cardiff' in the title, haunting the library, getting my friend Alan Beynon of Pontcanna Old Books to unearth ancient photos, battered maps and antiquarian books, and then scouring the internet for anything to do with the city. I found much more than I'd expected. It turns out that there are plenty of other obsessives out there. People whose interests include subterranean Cardiff (complete with maps and photos of the various nuclear bunkers and British telecom tunnels); trainspotter Cardiff (guides to the viewing of Diesel shunters and where the main lines run); arts Cardiff (music, exhibitions and what the seats are really like at UCI); and sports Cardiff ad infinitum (who won, will win, once won, ought to win and never could win plus weather reports, game reports, crowd reports, ball reports, racy dialogue and opinion collected down the pub). It's all there. Mary Sullivan's Newtown Association guide to the vanished Irish streets was fascinating. The Highways Department of Cardiff Council provided a detailed chronology covering the development of, among other things, Cardiff's water supply. Best of all were Patricia Sewell's painstaking transcriptions of John Hobson Matthew's nineteenth-century Cardiff Records. The internet transforms the way we research.

Later I became a tourist. I visited areas on foot, some amazingly for the first time, and tried to look at them through the eyes of a stranger to the city. With my partner, Sue, we took the bus tours, the guided tours, the boat trips, the walks, listened to the talks, toured the information centres, the exhibitions (notably Glenn Jordan's excellent old Butetown shows at the re-vamped Butetown History and Arts Gallery in Bute Street) and talked to passers-by. Most people we encountered imagined that we – clad in soft shoes and with cameras slung round our necks – were visitors from elsewhere. Was there someone called Bute who did things here, I'd ask? Bute? You mean the street. That's down the docks. You can get a train from Queen Street. When you bother to speak to them, Cardiffians are not at all the cold, recalcitrant urbanites they are often branded. They'll talk for hours.

The maps were best. At the central library ancient OS surveys of the burgeoning city proved an invaluable source in style and detail as to how it all had once been. There was a palpable excitement in using something drawn up in 1880 to guide a walk taken in 2001. Many things had changed, of course, but just as many had stayed the same.

Cardiff is a great place. Full of quirks, twists, turns, failures, magnificences, entertainments and excitements. It's small enough to hold but big enough to get lost in. Unlike larger metropolises it's almost possible to walk every street. It may not be redolently Welsh but it's not quite English either. It's wet. It's ethnic. It has lights and glass and masses of graffiti and rubbish dumped in hedges. You can holiday here and enjoy yourself thoroughly, so long as you don't stay for months. It may not yet be an Edinburgh or a Dublin but as a Celtic capital it's rising fast. And so long as the bouncy-castle municipal fireworks attitude is not allowed to run away with itself then the place has a fine European future to come.

Thanks are due to Mick Felton at Seren for the encouragement to turn the work into a book; to John Williams, John Briggs, Ifor Thomas, Lionel Fanthorpe, Steve Andrews, Dave Coombs and others for their suggestions and listening ears; to Sue for her constant help, unstinting support and encouragement, and for reading the whole thing more than once; to John Barnie for not being satisfied with the introductory article and for using further episodes in *Planet* as part of his Cityscapes series; and to all the visitors to *www.peterfinch.co.uk/cardiff* for their appreciation, comments, and suggested developments on the samples of this work posted there.

Why *Real Cardiff*? Because this is the real one, the one above, below and beyond the surface. It's also, dropping into the vernacular, *real Kardiff*, like. Don't read this in one sitting, dip. The plot is the shape of the city itself.

Out the window right now it's raining. Slow grey drizzle misting from the south west. Most of the book has been written under such conditions. Do you get used to it? Not really. But you do learn to live with it. That's how Cardiff is.

Peter Finch

INTRODUCTION

CARDIFF: CULTURE AND THE CITY

Somewhere in the middle of 2000, in one of those vox pop polls beloved of the tabloids, Cardiff got itself voted as 'most desirable destination' in the UK or something like that. "Cardiff is the new rock and roll", remarked one chubby-faced fresher from the East Midlands, displaying that innovative turn of phrase that only the English possess. "It's the place where it all happens." The description has stuck.

This is not a Welsh perception, naturally, far from it. For most of the Welsh population Cardiff remains a centre for permanent suspicion. It is regarded as too English, too distant, too flash, too fast, too large and far too anti-Welsh for many. Half of its population still think they live in the West Country. The rest don't care. Nevertheless, the excitement of being one of the newest of European capitals hangs light in the air. All you have to do is stand in the middle of Queen Street and look at the place. Something is going on – and going on at a considerable rate. But we're not quite sure what it is, are we, Mrs Jones?

Cardiff is a post-industrial city. There was a time – one which many who live here now can still remember – when the place stank permanently of coal, fume and ash. The vast East Moors steel works at its centre turned the air dark. Most of the south Wales valleys' coal output clanked its way through the city's heart to leave through its port. Cardiff was a place of smog and dark sunrises. But all that has gone, flattened and built on. The stonework has been washed and the streets are full of trees. Cardiff is now a university city of call-centres, leasing agents, insurance companies, utility providers, transport undertakings, plc head offices, banks and building societies. Cardiff is Wales's media centre – HTV, BBC, S4C and a host of satellite independents are all based in the city. Hardly anyone gets their hands dirty. There are lots of suits and cell-phones. It is a metropolis. These are rare in Wales.

Cardiff has been the Welsh capital since 1955 when it saw off Wrexham, Aberystwyth and a few other pale pretenders. It is also the site of the National Assembly despite the population overwhelmingly voting against having one in 1998. This piece of disingenuousness is shrugged off by many locals who have now embraced Welshness totally, rather in the style of Shirley Bassey, and can be observed flying the Ddraig Goch from the back of their taxis and sticking croeso on their shop front doors. Wales' new nation status has given Cardiffians an alternative to big brother next door England. Now there is also Europe. The English may be reluctant these days to say who they are but we, almost xenophobically, are not. Our sense of identity is vivid. We wear it well.

Nonetheless Cardiff does not feel a very Welsh place despite the bilingual street signs and the willingness of the Halifax Building society to take your money from you yn Gymraeg. The city is overtly multi-cultural with, for Wales, a large percentage of Asians, Afro-Caribbeans and significant enclaves from Somalia and Yemen. You can go out at night and listen to bhanghra music and there are cinemas that show nothing but Asian films. The University attracts Arabs and Iranians like a magnet and the centre streets can be full of dark, well dressed students with chador-clad women in tow. You can take a stroll down Queen Street of a Saturday and in quick succession be converted by charismatic Methodists, Moonies, Hare Krishnas and evangelical Muslims. Against this background it is difficult to believe that Cardiff is actually home to more Welsh speakers than anywhere except Gwynedd. When you leave home for the bright lights in Wales you don't go to Aberystwyth or Swansea, you come here.

Simple urban redevelopment, however, is not new or in any way unique to the Welsh capital. Both Swansea and Merthyr have been completely rebuilt and in Merthyr's case so well that the past there is now extremely hard to find. What is different in Cardiff is the combination of imagination and scale. Twenty years ago, well before identity took over as a driving force and the city slumbered with an old-fashioned museum, shows at the Sherman Theatre and films & art at an old school converted into an arts centre, the decision was taken. The money was found. One of Europe's largest inner-city regeneration projects was born.

St David's Hall, a genuine concert hall with a working acoustic shell, was erected opposite the old central library (later to become the short-lived Centre for the Visual Arts); the city centre was comprehensively pedestrianised and kitted out with the best shopping malls east of New York; and the Cardiff Bay Development Corporation was brought into being. This often controversial quango – now wound up, its work completed, its powers gone back to Cardiff County Council

– was given £2.5 billion pounds to redo what looks to the casual observer like the entire south of the City. The marketeers took over. What was the Docks became Cardiff Bay. This was much to the annoyance of locals who continue to call the place what they always have – Butetown.

£250,000 waterside penthouses have gone up in places redesignated with marketable names like Adventurers Quay and Rigarossa. A five-star hotel has been built on the waterfront (like the Hall also named St David's to capitalise on the reputation of a saint who never actually came here). A new grand boulevard – Lloyd George Avenue – has gone in behind the railway along which traffic now sweeps from the glittering city centre to the red brick Pier Head and the glories that will perhaps one day be the all-glass transparency of the National Assembly debating chamber. Soon the Wales Millennium Centre – Jonathan Adam's splendid slate and heritage coast concert hall, opera house, and international arts complex will open. Like a vast helmet it will dominate everything. The WMC will house, among others, the Welsh National Opera, The Urdd, Diversions Dance, The Academi and HiJinx Theatre. It will have a two metre high text composed by poet Gwyneth Lewis across its front celebrating our literary present. Already the area is thick with corporate headquarters. And there is copious supply of cafes, bars, gourmet-class restaurants, galleries, and open air coliseums.

All this is draped around the flats of Loudon Square and the tenements of Angelina Street. Take a walk up Bute Street. The wall retaining the last remnant of the Taf Vale Railway into the Bay has been chipped clean. The large white-letter and very legible graffiti painted there offering a welcome to INDEPENDENT TROPICAL CARDIFF is no more than dust. Beyond it are high-rises, domes and minarets. Under the shutters of the Beirut-battered shops are handbills which announce bands at The Packet and purifying Islamic lectures at the Alice Street mosque. The streets here have the highest rate of car crime anywhere in the city. How will the new, disparate communities get on with each other? Even the taxi drivers don't know.

Cardiff has been attracting change like a rolling snowball collects snow. Unlike Dublin or Edinburgh it has little hard history to hold it down. Ask what makes the City so exciting and the response will be unhesitating. You can drink here. But you can do that anywhere. Ah, but not with such variety, in such style, with such raging music and for such a continuous swath of time. Cardiff is the city that never sleeps. 24-hour supermarkets, 24-hour burger bars, 24-hour clubs.

The new bands that have made Wales so famous world-wide may not originate from Cardiff but they live and play here now. This is the land of shirts outside your trousers and studs in your nose. Hardly a week passes without a new café-bar or shining, minimalist drinkery starting up. Most are vast by traditional standards. The Wetherspoons Prince of Wales, a conversion of the old theatre of the same name, is the largest in Wales with space for a thousand drinkers. It is also the cheapest which has set off a welcome if very localised price war. At the height of the rush, when the place first opened and you couldn't get served for the crush, there was allegedly a chalked sign behind the bar reading "if you want to complain to the manager he's in Mulligans over the road". The Slurping Toad, Henrys, Bar Med, Ha-Has, Bar Cuba, Amigos, Stamps, The Pen and Wig are some of the latter day arrivals. Count them. None are relabelled traditional public houses. All are brand new ventures. The city's drinking provision climbs daily. According to the Council's web site there are currently 236 pubs, 293 off-licenses and 102 clubs. Not bad for a city whose centre was once known as Temperance Town.

The culture is driven by drink. The Millennium Stadium without a doubt a world standard attraction with its Thunderbirds Are Go sliding roof and unmistakable corner towers is encircled by bars equipped with machines that deliver half a dozen pints at one pull. Nothing new opens without a booze concession. Everything from the New Theatre to the Rugby World Cup runs on alcohol. But from where come the drinkers? Can the entire population of Cardiff be pissed all the time? The south Wales valleys provide a fair input but most of the regular punters come from Cardiff's estates and suburbs. Here, in the distant reaches of St Mellons, Rhiwbina and Whitchurch, last stop before the accent changes, the pubs have all switched to food and families. If you want life you go central. Check the Hippo, Po Na Na, Zeus, Latinos, Reds and the new Apocalypse. Living here can be pretty much as depicted in Justin Kerrigan's *Human Traffic*.

It's not all low life. Cardiff does offer its middle-class, cultural elite something – it always has. Opera at the New, Martin Tinney selling Harry Holland, The Albany moving Kyffin Williams, good orchestras at St David's Hall, and some of the best public art anywhere in the world. And after the failure of the Centre for the Visual Arts the National Museum of Wales' galleries now reassert themselves. They do a good job. Chapter is fine (it's free) but is nowhere near the centre. Oriel was the best but that's long gone.

Over the years the writing community has not served the city as well as it could have. There is still not as much identifiable local literary fog as there is, for example, in Swansea. Not enough focus, not much status, too little style. Dannie Abse came from here and celebrates this in his books but he's a *éminence grise* living in London now. Unlike Dublin, Edinburgh, Newcastle, Huddersfield and other regional centres Cardiff has little pull in the literary world at large. Chapter hosts regular readings such as Seren's *First Thursday* and Jon Gower's *Speakeasy* but the writers don't like the place much and the Centre's focus is usually on other things. The Café Europa writers have their heads above the parapet, just. The *New Welsh Review* was edited in the city but it's now moved. Red Sharks Press has died, and Parthian Books, one of the great new lights has gone to Cardigan. There are readings in centre pubs and a flock of writers' circles but that's no different than it is, say, in Newport. In literary terms Cardiff has spent far too long exhibiting Victoria Park values, harking back after Billy the Seal, Clarksies pies and pints of dark. Only John Williams with his genuinely realistic *Five Pubs, Two Bars And A Nightclub* and his novel, *Cardiff Dead* has attempted to catch hold of what's really going on. Frank Hennessey and his constant celebration of our most un-Welsh accent has a lot to answer for. But there are signs, out there, of a revival. London publishers are starting to scratch at the city's surface. Anna Davis, proud of her Cardiff origins, uses the place as background for her thrillers, Lloyd Robson's *Cardiff Cut* roars through the streets as a piece of superb literary grease, and Grahame Davies's Welsh language verse takes the place to bits. Look and you'll find more. Sean Burke, John Harrison, Bill James. The city's literary reputation is on the up.

Standing at the Penarth end of the Cardiff Bay Barrage – the dam that has turned the bird friendly mud flats either into a swamp or a world-class boating lake, depending on who you listen to – I can see a glistening, high-rise city full of flash and street art, glass and cash. It's great to say I belong. The light here is different. But there are pockets of backsliding. Progress never moves forward like a wall. The Bute Dock, a showpiece of municipal-run regeneration with the UCI cinema and club complex at its south and the pagoda roof of County Hall along its western edge, is by now showing strong signs of neglect. The brick walkways are overgrown, the cast-iron railings have mostly been uprooted and hurled into the sea. There is a sign which reads WARNING – TOXIC BLUE GREEN ALGAE MAY BE PRESENT IN THIS DOCK.

DO NOT ENTER THE WATER. And beyond there are others who seem determined not to join the great new society. The vast lumpen enclaves of Ely and, to a lesser extent, Llanrumney remain walled cities with their own cultures running in oblivion to what's going on elsewhere. They support Cardiff City, a team bobbing the league's lower echelons and with a reputation for supporter violence not usually witnessed in Wales. Their traditional culture makes few concessions to the new wealth around them. What, here, does street art, café culture and grand opera actually mean?

Cardiff is not all culture. Millennium Stadium and our rugby obsession apart, the top attraction in recent years according to official figures is not the now tragically demolished Industrial and Maritime Museum or even the engaging St Fagans but Harry Ramsden's, the chip shop on the waterfront, which pulled more than 500,000 visitors last year. Stand outside there in the summer and you'll be served by a rubber wheeled tourist train and carriages which toots between the Norwegian Church and the Barrage for an amazing £2.00 a go. At last the centre of Wales has made it as Disneyland. Soft-shoed Americans in drip-dry slacks and baseball caps drift along the sidewalks. Cardiff has become a true holiday destination. Billy the Seal would be proud.

MEWN

Coke legals shirt-tail bay boy whoppa cwpan cymraeg Korea siapan mall sneakers ice devils 5.00 am suit and armband Koran pack glass massaged glass fat arse plane crap train Tom Jones Iwan Bala Angharad anything dragon bluebirds flags café money Mermaid Mallard's Reach Flying Trout Hemmingway Heaven Bosun's Avenue Atlantic Wharf Leisure Village Glass Waving slate stacked the Russell Goodway Memorial Roundabout cycle way speed stripe pile of bricks euro-time multi-screen disposable glory future proof young assembling assembly absolutely.

MAS

Victoria Park coal and steel mild pale Harlech Sophia Shakin Donleavy night Philanderer Jim Callaghan corporation west of England red light Vic Parker aright skip ship matey pint of sarsaparilla 10.30 Spanish club afternoon valley day Portland stone Metal Street black mortar Taf Vale Tom Jones Shirl walking Crockherbtown Caribbean red light bike overtime Christian marching salvaged beam engines Pink Floyd flood trolley Estonian Polski coffee bar Italiano fog Welcome to Cardiff General that's the Pearl Building do not walk in the gutter sorry.

EAST

NEWPORT ROAD

At the east end of Queen Street, beyond the railway that climbs through what's left of the once booming Cardiff valleys, is Newport Road. This is the old highway which runs like an arrow the dozen or so miles to Cardiff's almost-forgotten neighbour, Newport. Built to ship iron from the mouth of the Usk, Newport has little glory save the heritage of its unique transporter bridge. And even that got located as Cardiff for Rank's 1959 film *Tiger Bay*. At their end the highway is called Cardiff Road, a bright prospect you'd imagine, but most Newportians resent the flash and dominance of the Welsh capital. That's what's wrong with it, they perversely insist, it's Welsh.

Newport Road moves out from Cardiff centre through a rush of merchant banks, high-rise consultancies and outposts of the multi-nationals which govern the western world. Jammed incongruously here on a road of such permanent haste is the Institute for the Blind. This 50s glass palace sells large print books, bells which tell their owners when it's raining and devices which let them fill their tea-cups just to the top. Behind its frontage is the Boucher Hall. Here, in 1965, Geraint Jarman, Finch, David Callard and one Wyn Islwyn Davies, now vanished from creative sight like Arthur Cravan[1], mounted the first ever *second aeon* poetry reading. This was in front of an audience of ten friends and five strangers, rattling loudly in a room designed for several hundred more.

The road, as it stretches on, away from the city, is ranged with hefty Victorian merchants' residences. These are now converted almost entirely to *one-stop, satellite TV in all rooms, vacancies, we welcome*

construction workers, bar, secure lock-up car park at back, two harp WTB recommended, if no answer knock at side-door hotels. Bronte, Blue Dragon, Courtlands, Glenmor, Imperial, Metropole, Marlborough. Groups of men – shopfitters from Bristol, trench-diggers from Wexford, electricians from Dudley – wearing check shirts and calf-high suede boots gather on the pavements here each night and wonder which way it is to the lights. I brought the Czech poet Miroslav Holub once. An overnight stop after his reading at the University. The rain was sheeting down as it does in Hollywood films depicting New York. We entered the foyer to find buckets catching leaks and a fall of water rolling its way from landing to hall. "Like home," he smiled. "I'll like it here."

Back of the main road are the hostels for reforming alcoholics, the doss joints for the homeless and charity refuges for drug victims on the cure and the ragged embittered who just don't care. The pavements are wide and cars park right across them. If you're pushing a pram, sod you. In the long stretch beyond St Peter's Rugby Club – once the only place in all of East Cardiff where you could drink after 10.30 pm – I'm accosted by a rancorous wreck making kokutsu-dachi[2] with an empty cider tin in one hand and a Guinness bottle in the other. "You bastard," he moans. The weak, wet rage of the destroyed. Terry, another long-term delinquent and loony stopped here with his wife in a wheel-chair and played harmonica to passing traffic before passing out. No one stopped. She's dead now. He's inside.

Towards the funeral home use turns to residential care for the elderly. Front lawns are lost below white gravel, flowers are in baskets. There are bright signs and powder paper faces peering out through window corners. In the sixties I had a flat just beyond here. Two rooms stuffed with fervent bohemianism Visions of Johanna, Roadrunner, Doors of Perception, Duluoz, dharma, Bomb Culture, Needle of Death. Real needles in the gardens now, when I look. The road goes on. It always did.

BROADWAY

The first few hundred yards of Broadway at the town end are called Four Elms Road, after the trees that once stood here. Beyond, religion stakes an early claim. Just past the site of Longcross Barracks (now an outbuilding of the increasingly defunct Royal Infirmary) rises Trinity

Methodist with its hardwood doors, flowers, glass and billboards offering punters "a wide range of mid-week activities for all ages". Next door is an imposing but derelict Wesleyan pile, once used for God, then the BBC and now abandoned completely. Broadway itself begins rather uneventfully at the traffic lights next to The Clifton, the first of the street's many pubs. And there are quite a few. Even by working-class Cardiff standards Broadway is well served. A long time ago I made the mistake here, when drinking with Ray Smith, the late Welsh actor, of attributing his apparent lack of UK national success to his status as a south Wales valley boy. "It's not fashionable", I told him, "Being Welsh. Doesn't work". Smith, a small man but with a rich commanding voice in the style of Richard Burton, erupted. I should have expected it, I know. What did I imagine he'd do? Agree? Then, as these things do, in public houses after several beers, indignation moved from personal to general, seeping out and away from the table at which we sat. "Welsh. What do you know about it? This place doesn't even stock Welsh beer," complained Smith loudly, holding hard to the nationalist line. "Doesn't exist," interrupted the landlord. "What about Felinfoel?" It was an irrefutable statement. The regulars watched impassively as we were escorted out.

Before the city and its buildings encroached and the land here was still open, marshy field Broadway was known as Green Lane. Its exact line holds, even on the very earliest of Cardiff maps. That's one of the great discoveries of local history: the courses of rivers may be changed, lakes may be filled, land can be drained, buildings rise, houses fall, and habitation can move about like an amoeba but the lines of the main thoroughfares remain stable, most of them, just where they've always been.

By present day standards Broadway is not broad at all, although I guess that in the days of green lanes it might have been thought so. Two carts could pass each other here unhindered. No doubt they did this at the kink in the road where the massage parlour and Jerks black, gold chain and t-shirt café now stand. Most of the shops are either places which reprocess second hand cookers, bedroom furniture and carpets or are boarded up and falling down. After a hundred years of rain and neglect the housing stock, which went up towards the end of the nineteenth century, is on its last legs. In between those buildings that remain habitable have sprung small trading enterprises of the kind you just don't see in city centres – Lalazar Halal Take Away, the Tattoo Studio, the Saroosh Fish Bar, charity shops, a TV aerial erection outfit, places selling chrome fitments for motor bikes, heavy metal amplifiers and, in the middle of it all, Reg Braddick's bike shop, a legend to cyclists everywhere.

At the far end things get rougher and women with shaved heads and tattoos on their necks start to appear. The Locomotive, now all satellite TV lounge and Karaoke, used to house the city's best sixties folk club. Dominic Behan sang here, accompanied by a whole tray of single malts. Bright women with English accents and Appalachian mountain dulcimers held the cord jeaned crowds in awe. And here the Hennesseys got an early taste of public acclaim. These were the glory days before Cardiffness got into their songs and certainly before half their lyrics turned Cymraeg. Then their music was unashamed Irish. It's a flavour that hangs on in Broadway today.

Outside The Locomotive someone passes in a car which has all four indicator lights flashing and a woop woop alarm going off under the bonnet. Nobody takes the slightest notice. There's not a flicker among the two women with wheeled shopping carts or the Asian family stringing their way along bearing red Kwik-Save carrier bags. The road pitches on past The Bertram, the Labour Club, the second-hand record shop (now simply a second hand shop, no blues, no rock, no mouldy unplayable Frank Sinatra or Funk Hits in Hi-Fi, full now of ill-shaped wardrobes and stacked settees), past the cod-Elizabethan boarded-up edifice on the corner of Blanche Street, and the New Dock Tavern, to finally rejoin roaring Newport Road at The Royal Oak.

When I passed the Oak had an Irish flag flying from one upper window and, rather incongruously, a Canadian one from another. This is the pub that has a working boxing gym upstairs and a ground-floor ultra-traditional bar dedicated to the memory of Peerless Jim Driscoll. When Alexander Cordell came here researching for his novel about the boxer the locals he spoke to were all certain they'd have cameo roles in the great man's next historical adventure. The Oak is one of Cardiff's best known unreconstructed Brains pubs. It exudes that welcoming dark, smoky, scuff and spit atmosphere which is utterly absent from family pubs and completely alien to the light wood and aluminium favoured by drinking's latter-day fans. The Oak's band room at the back can be a brilliantly furious sweat shop. The Socialist Worker Party and other people's political manifestations of the far left meet here over roll-ups and dark ale. A few writers gather in the lounge. It's a friendly place. When carrying out what could laughingly be called research for this piece I tried to get myself a seat on the long bench in the scuff and spit front bar. Take in the atmosphere, that's what you do. "Could you move up, do you think?" I asked a big guy in builder's boots. The giant satellite TV screen above was showing football, what else. – "No," he muttered. "I bloody well carn't".

CITY ROAD

City Road is a run-down inner-Cardiff city thoroughfare. It's thick with car showrooms, Asian restaurants, Spar 24-hour groceries and boarded, abandoned shops. It runs from the student land of Cathays, through the five-way death junction of City, Albany, Richmond, Crwys and Macintosh, to the closed and decaying Royal Infirmary, where the Longcross once stood, on Newport Road. It's a street everyone knows but hardly anyone loves. Up until the middle of last century it was known as Heol-y-Plwcca after the gallows field at its northern end. Here, in a plot known as 'the Cut Throats', more or less where the Road has its junction with Albany, stood the town gibbet. Nearby were plots called Cae Budr (the defiled field), Plwcca Halog (the unhallowed plot), and Pwll Halog (the unhallowed pool). Today they've got side streets built across them and are happily called Strathnairn, Glenroy and Keppoch. The grimness has been vanquished, buried under backgarden clay and foundation, forgotten. There's a bakers, a Lebanese fast-food and an army surplus store selling Italian combat jackets, imitation pistols, folding shovels and camouflage nets. For a brief time City Road was called Castle Road,

after Roath Castle, the former great house which now runs bowls, drinking, the Night-Writers creative writing group and tennis as The Mackintosh Institute. But since Cardiff had a bigger and more important Castle elsewhere names had to change. Innocuous, anodyne *City Road* the thoroughfare became. In the old photos it has trolleys and trams running down it and the street lamps are gas. But the buildings look more or less as they do now – little development, few add-ons, no rebuilds. Under the onslaught of more than a hundred years of south Wales drizzle City Road has simply crumbled slightly. The gloss has gone from its surfaces. Today it is seedy, edgy, slightly wrecked, and, yes, exciting – all by turns.

Cardiff's 1980s live-writing manifestation, *Cabaret 246*, began here, in the upstairs room of the Roath Park. Cab was an outgrowth of Chris Torrance's famous *Adventures In Creative Writing* night class held in the Department of Continuing Education at Cardiff University. Torrance's bohemian beat generation meets the south Wales rain approach had a wide acceptance. Everyone from the hippest of street punks to retired policemen passed through the bearded, woollen-capped bard's hands. Half of Torrance's appeal was that he listened to what his students had to say. The rest lay in the sheer breadth and openness of his recommended texts. Torrance's required reading sprinted from ancient Japanese haiku to contemporary New York dope celebrations via Blake, Pope, Coleridge, Corso and the whole of the UK small press scene. People signed on for his year long class and twelve months later they signed on again. He retired in 2001, victim of form filling and stifling bureaucracy. Literature loses again.

The first Cab was a public performance of the Torrance class output put on in the best venue they could find. This turned out to be upstairs in The Roath Park, an obscure, out of city-centre pub with poor parking but the right rent and the right beer. Given the literary antecedents of the area the choice wasn't all that bad. In the sixties emerging Anglo-Welsh poets had staggered and shouted in the nearby curry houses. At a time when the city had little better to offer,

J.P. Donleavy came here for six popadums and a meat Madras. Members of Cardiff's earlier poetry performance platform – *No Walls* – although they never actually performed in City Road spent a fair amount of time in its pubs, clubs and cafs. Geraint Jarman, David Callard, Huw Morgan, Fred Daly and I were often seen at the Bongla Bhashi or the Curry Mohal – although, curiously, never at the pub then known as *Poets Corner*. This was where I tried to sell copies of my sixties literary magazine, *second aeon*, to hard-bitten fag and beer working men who suggested that I was not only not as good as Wordsworth but also a Nancy. But that's another story.

Cabaret 246 – as a performance poetry organisation – grew out of that first night at the Roath Park. Torrance's class boasted some pretty powerful voices, although they had yet to learn their trade. Ifor Thomas, Tôpher Mills, and John Harrison were all Torrance protégés. Where did I fit in? As a 70s sound poet used to performing to empty halls and rooms containing only the organiser and his sandwiches, Torrance's invitation to take turn as a guest was welcome. I did my Cobbinesque best. No one understood a word.

Literary events, of course, do not need patrons. The writers themselves are generally audience enough. With little or no promotion Cabaret 246 began to attract the crowds. It was throwing up the same kind of outrage and invention as did its famous precursor in pre-WWI Zurich. Smoke machines mixed with chain saws. There were domestic appliance percussion orchestras, strobe lit dancing, verse delivered while wearing gas masks, books ripped into paper chases, and poems set on fire. Sound poetry re-emerged from its late fifties doldrum for another brief blur of glory. The short story took

new life as a bar stool pastime. Writers jostled to out invent and out perform each other. Torrance, file in bag and tea flask in pocket, watched from the corner. For a brief time Cab was white hot.

Change, as ever, is the driver. It is a fact of life when renting pub rooms that on your most important night for decades you'll turn up and find the landlord, through some long standing and utterly incomprehensible arrangement, has already let the space to someone else. You'll be there at 8.30 with your props, your audience and your special guest bought in with Arts Council help and travelled all the way from Edinburgh to be faced with a lounge rearranged to resemble a board room and every chair taken by beer drinking hobbyists at their AGM. And so it was. The landlord moved on to The Flora in Cathays where there was no space and the incoming Roath Park tenant wanted no further truck with writers. Cab shifted to better, wilder and much more destructive things at Chapter, the Gower in Gwenith Street and then the city centre Four Bars. City Road returned to its regular cycle of quiet violence, 24 hour shopping, loonies, drunks and dopos. In recent times it has become the centre of Cardiff author lloyd robson's *Making Sense of City Road* project which merges photograph, found text and verse. It's on the web at *www.lloydrobson.co.uk*. Check it out.

Writers' Guidelines

A pamphlet of poems and a hard-backed novel will accelerate at the same speed when you chuck them down a stairwell.

Fiction always ends

Tall writers are older than short ones

Poems grow spontaneously overnight

You can learn most of what you need from a book simply by carrying it about.

Fixing buggered metre is as easy as unplugging the sink

Say hello often enough and you'll soon be famous

Write by saying you have.

Make it up

Why not.

CLAUDE ROAD

In the early 1980s when VHS won the battle against Betamax and Blockbuster Video had not yet taken over the entire rental world there was a small video outlet opposite the Chinese take-away on the corner of Claude Place and Albany Road. It made money on kids stuff, thrillers, science fiction and martial arts movies. In its window it had a hand scuffed sign which read 'Absolutely no rental to anyone with an address in Claude or Connaught Roads.' The front gardens here were often thick with junked mattresses and wrecked wardrobes. The rears of electric cookers could be seen behind unwashed front room windows. Black plastic refuse bags lay like seals below overgrown hedges. This was a territory of transients. Rooms. Flats. Victorian houses fragmented. Communal kitchens. Dark halls full of billowing junk mail. Stairs with no carpets. Overgrown gardens where no one went.

Claude Road, along with the vast Claude Hotel which runs to the back of it, were named after Claude, the third son of Charles Henry Williams of Roath Court, on whose land they were built. They went up in the 1890s as part of Cardiff's great industrial expansion east. Terraced town houses with room enough for full-size Victorian families, gardens of beech and privet, mews to the rear. Respectability. Fanthorpe reckoned that the land once held a Viking settlement but that a millennium of farming had wiped the ground record clean. It was all hard-core now.

Lionel Fanthorpe, author, priest, leather-clad presenter of Channel Four's *Fortean TV*, and New-Age renaissance man, has been a

Cardiffian for more than twenty years. He lives at the quieter end of Claude Road in a house which has the same waste-ground look about its front garden as everyone else's. Above the door, in flaky not quite perfect letters, is the house name – *Rivendell*. A Tolkein marker to the hippie era it had been when Fanthorpe first moved in. I'd come round to see him for guidance on the holy wells of the district but he seemed a little distant from these touchable mysteries. More important were the Maltese family, a few doors up, whose mother had died and had Lionel administer the funeral. They were currently shifting painted-plaster eagles, flowering shrubs in dustbins and quarter-size Madonnas into their tiny front garden as a sort of memorial. Would anyone now vandalise these treasures? They might.

Lionel moved to Cardiff from Norfolk, chasing work. He'd taken on the headship of a difficult comprehensive school in Ely, a post he then held for ten years until his other pursuits blossomed to such an extent that he'd been forced to give up. On his web site *www.lionel-fanthorpe.com* he lists himself as 'self-employed actor, raconteur, singer/song-writer, general entertainer, TV presenter, writer, broadcaster, lecturer, tutor and consultant.' Quite a cv. What he doesn't say is that the writing is either Church-in-Wales happy-clappy end evangelicising or mystery solving tomes about magnetic hills, haunted houses, demons, buried ufos and lost treasures. Add to that the fact that he's a third Dan at judo, an ordained priest, a qualified weight trainer and rides a Harley-Davidson Electra-glide (currently locked in the garage which vandals have at least once tried to burn down) and you get a man who doesn't fit any of the regular categories. Where does the money come from? A trickle from his TV programmes repeating on digital, more soon from a new series on castles, but the bulk from GCSE tutoring. Maths is his speciality. Accuracy. Clarity. A subject with rules which work.

It's a glorious day. Street cats lounge on window ledges. We sit in Rivendell's front room with the drapes closed. Patricia, Lionel's wife and co-conspirator, brings in tea. Looking a little like Captain Birdseye and exuding bonhomie and enthusiasm Lionel explains his priesthood. He has no parish, he's non-stipendiary, a sort of religious locum. He works Sundays to cover absences. Weekdays he hunts aliens and unravels mysteries. Teaches. And writes. He goes in for writathons, producing complete novels, plays and vast sequences of metrically accurate verse in single overnight sittings. Charity drives him, the good of the cause is more important than the fame. He is used to pressure. He can churn. In the fifties he was a staff writer for Badger Books, a pulp-paperback science-fiction publisher, which relied on sheer volume to stay in business. TV had yet to take over people's lives. When you were bored you didn't gape and drink, you read. Badger stacked them high and sold them cheap. Half-a-crown would get you a luridly-covered Fanthorpe original where Henderson and Caruthers fought aliens on Mars or chased spies through the clouds of Venus. To keep his output at required levels Lionel would dictate his fiction into a portable recorder and then send the tapes out for transcription. He knew exactly how many reels equalled 50,000 words, a book's length, and when the final tape ran towards its finish the tale had, somehow, to neatly conclude. A favourite device was the Flazgaz Heat Ray which sat in a red box with the words 'Not To Be Used In Any Circumstances' emblazoned across its front. In a Badger Books' closing paragraphs Henderson (with support from upstanding Caruthers) would often open the container, remove the device, and blast the marauding monsters into oblivion. The Flazgaz may have been a terrible machine but it always worked. The world would again be saved.

Fortean TV rocketed Lionel to fame. His TV image was perfect – white beard, dog collar, black clothed, leather clad – the priest who looked at the world's underside, checked its strangeness, uncovered its mysteries. Kids would approach him at motorway service stations and ask for an autograph. The strange and deranged would bring him their obsessions. How do you handle the seriously upset? I ask. Take the Christian approach. Don't hurt. Don't ridicule. Suggest alternative solutions. Be bland. Become the lead shield around their faulty intellectual radiation. Does it happen much? Now and then.

Lionel is one of King Arthur's Quest Knights, of course, the honour bestowed in a front room in Ely. Do you run into Arthur much these days? I ask. It's a reasonable question. I saw him last, says Lionel, wearing his long white robes, with his sword and his badge of office clutched to him, lying fast asleep outside Cardiff Central Railway Station. On one of the benches. As one of his loyal knights I suppose I should have woken him but I let him doze. Cardiff's hippy layer stays solid. Lionel strides across it. Bold and unflagging. An unlikely remnant. Genuinely good.

Walking back up the road there's music leaking from upstairs bedrooms – where it was once the Incredible String Band now it's Gorky's Zygotic Mynci. New faces, same territory. Someone has a leaded-glass rainbow in their lounge window. The sun goes in through it spraying coloured light across the wood-chipped wall. Is this the original or a re-invention? Nothing's new. Never was.

DEANS FARM

Coming up through what were once open fields I pass Billy Block relaying his front lawn with upended bricks. He hasn't got it quite level and the rain pools to the lower right. The mortar smears across the hard red surface. No matter. The weather will wear it in time. Billy is laying re-cycled local house, dug from the clay pits under Colchester Avenue Sainsburys and fired in the long gone Roath Pottery and Brickworks. They used these to turn Deans Farm into Southminster Road in 1924. This triangle of streets – Southminster, Axminster, Sturminster, Newminster, lies tight between three churches – the ancient St Margaret's, the Parish Church of Roath; the United Reform Church; and the Plymouth Brethren's Minster Road Gospel Hall. You'd image that at such close proximity they'd compete in their chasing after righteous souls, but they don't. The most I've seen is the Gospel Hall mini-bus ferrying aged worshipers in and the black-robed St Margaret's vicar flowing past, good book in hand.

Deans Farm house, Ysgubor Fawr, stood where Billy Block's garage now is. Its 117 Acres of pasture abutting Ty Mawr, the next farm's 101. This was the heart of the old Roath Village. The church, the manor house of Roath Court, cottages, the farms, the Lleici running right through them. Roath Court House, with a grand porch added in 1956[3], is now a funeral home. Outside, snuck tight against the famous white wall, is a grade two listed GPO phone box. Still working. Used at night by lost European lorry drivers and kids with cell phones needing a shelter. Owen John Thomas tells me that the swell of earth on which the church is built suggests that there was once an iron age fort here. No proof but a satisfying theory. When the global waters rise the Church will stay dry.

Southminster is a slow curve with dual carriage way width pavements and the narrowest cambered roadway anywhere in East Cardiff. I asked the kerb-layers, there in the 1990s to turn the gentle matchbox-high edges into tyre breaking eight inch cliffs, why they didn't widen the road, given its rat run status of fast taxis and hacked-off commuters beating the Newport Road lights. Can't be done, mate. All the services are below this pavement. Pipes and that. Wouldn't stand the weight. Too near the top.

But it's a quiet street. At the St Margaret's end the Ty Mawr old people's home occupies the site of the former Llys Ddu farm house. This great house started life in the sixteenth century and lasted until 1967. I can just about remember it, walking home from school and using Southminster as a short-cut, trying hard to enjoy a surreptitious Consulate Menthol, cool as a mountain stream, didn't taste like tobacco, still made me dizzy.

I moved here in the late 1970s, no longer a small magazine editor but still encumbered with a life of books and papers. The removers charged extra for the humping. Print is heavy. They advised against stacking the books in the loft. Timbers won't take it, you need proper metal shelves for this. Do a bit of reading, do you? I likes cowboy books myself. They put the stuff in the converted garage at the back. A long studio-like extension built by the former owner[4], a bit-player architect, occasional entrepreneur and wide boy. His approach was style without substance. The stripped doors had no furniture. They hung into their architraves with single screws. For speed water pipes were routed up the walls' cavities. The shower extract-fan blew wet air into the roof space and rotted the timbers. The boxed-in bath lacked base support. When you stood up your foot went right through the outlet pipe. Streaming water poured through the ceiling into the dining room below.

The books line the south walls now. Wooden shelves, more volumes than Roath Park Public Library: a life of beat fiction, world poetry, avant garde art, the lit of Wales and books on the endless business of making books. Wall upon wall. Folders, brochures, neat pamphlets, slim magazines, irregular mimeographed sheets corner-stapled, slick Pronto-print fold-overs, chapbooks, spine finished vols made with carpet glue and two house bricks, hard backs bound professionally, sewn folios, spiral-held new age wonders. Publishing goes in circles. It says what it needs to. Repeats itself. And in case we didn't hear, says it again.

Fewer poets visit Southminster than previous places I've lived. My days as a small literary publisher ended in 1975. The Americans treck here less, spending their vacations searching the source of *second aeon*[5], trying the find the guy who published William Wantling, Douglas Blazek, Allen Ginsberg, William Burroughs, Charles Plymell, Clayton Eshleman, Larry Eigner, Robert Bly, Bob Cobbing,

Cid Corman, and bill bissett in that place, Cardiff, Wales, in the swinging sixties. Who was he? Don't ring my bell at night now. Don't know I'm here.

I stare out at the giant gunnera growing like a Triffid in the damp shady bottom of my pencil slim garden. Each year it gets bigger. Taller than my reach this year, with leaves at least five foot across. The books are how-tos, information sections for national guides, book reviews, critical pieces, self-publishing advice for starters, poems. Haven't given that up. My stuff. Still do those.

In the lane at the back that separates Southminster from what used to be Deanfield Terrace and is now Albany Road someone has dumped a stolen Escort and set it on fire. The torched vehicle explodes in a blast of yellow-red, vicious heat. The buckets of water I sling on my burning roof do nothing. The house fills with rolling smoke. It takes the brigade to fix it. A breathing-mask clad female fire fighter waving a foaming hose orders me from my roof. Inside the fire team leader takes me aside. He wants me to stop me fussing and get out of the way of the men arriving with helmets, hatchets and hoses. Write a bit, do you, he says, indicating with his arm the book stacks wavering behind the smoke. I nod. So do I. I'm half way through a novel. We get a lot of spare time between shouts. Any advice you could offer me? Stick at it, I say, you'll get there. Behind us the flames are rapidly subdued.

The whole episode is over almost as fast as it began. It helps living five minutes from Fire Service HQ. Roof timbers creak. The insurance fixes everything, even the smell. Lost a few books, nothing valuable. The bulk remain. A wall of insulation in the heart of Roath Village. It's always been a warm place.

THE FOUR ELMS

At a point roughly half way between the Julian Hodge Building, Cardiff's first high-rise, and The Royal Oak, at the end of Broadway, lies Elm Street. This unprepossessing terrace of workers' housing put up at the end of the last century is one of the few places in Cardiff where the grey light of south Wales has been ignored. The residents have painted the render on their frontages in Mediterranean Technicolor. Greek orange, crab pink, sky blue, dust avocado, Italian cream, tooth-pick red. No sludge, not a sign of mould, the windowsills are full of flower boxes, hanging tubs and ceramic

butterflies. The street has seen innovation before. When the poet and architect Ifor Thomas lived here he installed sunken baths, moved doors and rebuilt walls. But you had to take care, this was old Cardiff. Press hard, he told me, and you could push your hand through the plaster right into next door.

There once were elms here. Four of them, shown on the OS maps of 1789, growing roughly where Lower Clifton Street intersects with Broadway. There was a mile stone, still there in 1969, gone now. The pub called after the trees, The Four Elms, now gloriously renamed and repainted as The Yellow Kangaroo, hosted a writers' gathering for a short time in its life. In a little-used backroom which held the pub's water cistern and a collection of aged accoutrements belonging to the local Order of the Buffalo (a less well financed, considerably less able and utterly less secret working-class version of the Masons) writers would gather to exchange ideas, read poems, criticise each other's work and drink. The beat writer, Gerald Nicosia, visited here with his mother. You could tell that's who she was because she wore a large lapel badge saying so. AUTHOR'S MOTHER. She led the applause vigorously every time the great man spoke. Actually Gerry fitted in well. He was short, Italian looking, and displayed a tenacious enthusiasm for his own work. He'd written *Memory Babe*, a critical biography of Jack Kerouac for Penguin and was on a roll. What he was now doing in the back streets of Cardiff, mom in tow, talking to a bunch of wannabes, some of whom didn't even own typewriters was anyone's guess. Gerry read his own verse, faux-beat stuff, thick with bohemian allusion and then dipped into his Kerouac to tell us about Denver, Jack and Neil and Carolyn and Allen and make us all want to go straight out, shove a few benzedrine inhalers down our throats and stay up all nite. He had to stop every now and then as drinkers in the bar below us used the gents. This made the cistern flush noisily. We cheered. Mom had a great time. She'd never been to Wales before and was now convinced that we were as literary a bunch as her son's cohorts in Chicago. Outside Welsh rain rattled the windows. Someone filled a missing pane with a plastic bag. Gerry did not have any copies of his books with him for resale. A refreshing sign of literary don't care or one of earlier success? Who knows. Shortly after that the pub went up-market installing satellite TV and pumping non-stop sports into every drinking nook and beer consuming cranny. Half the pubs in Cardiff were doing the same. The Frog and Toad, The Duck and Donkey, The Useless Lettuce, The Newt and Corkscrew, The Pissed Potato. The writers moved on. The world of poetry, beatniks, and buffalo, always suspect, changed again.

LAKE

There are a number of ways to drain land. Time-honoured is the drainage ditch. Put in a network, take the water slowly somewhere else. More costly, but neater, are deep-dug land drains: pipes that let the excess enter the sewers. But if resource or logistics are problematic then making a feature of the dampness might be the best route forward. The malarial bog which occupied both sides of the Lleici south of where the Lisvane and Llanishen reservoirs now stand had always been resistant to solution. So why not make it a lake? In the autumn it was mostly that anyway. This part of Cardiff was Bute land, vast acres of it. A commendable solution. But the Marquis was not given to philanthropy without purpose. Bute knew that in order to build and sell high value property you need to provide amenity. In 1887 he offered 103 acres of upper Roath to the Corporation, got this matched by 18 acres from

Lord Tredegar, and established the chain of public spaces that still run in a green line out from the city's heart. The spaces were centred on what was to eventually become Roath Park Lake and Botanical Gardens. It took the Corporation several thousands of pounds and a further seven years to dig, drain, pave and plant this Victorian splendour, the gardens opening in 1894, water at their centre. The imposing

properties Bute built along its flanks, some of the most imposing Cardiff had yet seen, sold magnificently well.

Over the years the Lake developed its own mythology. Tram routes led to it. Trolley bus terminuses were set at its entrance. Rare plants were planted in its gardens. There were bandstands, ice-cream parlours, elegant walkways, rock gardens, rose terraces, waterfalls, paddling pools, maple plantings, and boats. Loads of boats. The lake was filled with rowers you could hire, pedal boats for kids, motor launches for those who wanted the tour with low effort, barges for the swimmers, model yachts for the seafaring, and for the rest – ducks, swans, geese, fish and islands. Five artificial mysteriosos were created at the north end. After his single gig in Cardiff during the early seventies Jimi Hendrix was reputed to have woken up, stoned, on one of them. Where am I, man? Don't worry bro, you're in a foreign land.

There's something about this thin waterway which attracts people more than the coast does. Try walking round it on a Boxing Day and you'll be lucky to find yourself a free couple of yards. The pathways will be packed with scarf and coat clad Cardiffians pumping their systems free of turkey sludge, towing their kids on new bikes/scooters/skateboards/in-line rollers/electric shoes/zippo trainers. And there'll be dogs too: pooches, Alsatians, lap-dogs, yappy mongrels, and old-timers with smiles in their tails.

Lake myths

Atomic
Full of gold
Horse and cart buried at centre
Fish all die
Tunnel
Big bivalves
Cyncoed house drains exhale here
Money
Snakes
Suds
Lady of Lake and silver sword
Floaters

There's not that much of Roath Park Lake in Cardiff literature. To correct this Jarman and I planned a reading which would have the poets on the islands shouting their verse by megaphone to assembled fans in deckchairs strewn along the banks. Didn't come off. Jan Leslie Olsen, lunatic Norwegian follower of H.P. Lovecraft, borrowed a row boat in 1968 and drifted oarless along the side of the  promenade shouting out his mad stanzas. Rimbaud of the Welsh capital. Ignored by passers-by. Small children threw bread.

Periodically the Lake gets drained and the ducks retreat to the decreasing slop of water at the long body's centre. The waterfall at the south end cascades down a series of low steps from the ice-cream stall, seat and flower-box strewn promenade (just like the sea side) to the rose garden and botanic adventures below. I climbed in once and found the step shelves full of coin. Visitors making a wish threw away their money. No history, no tradition, no bent pins nor bushes covered with votive scraps of cloth. This was a unilateral, popular solution to life's difficulties. Parks are places where you can sort your problems, the swan is the resident oracle, the waterfall the epicentre of suburban dreams.

Glory be to Bute, no one's yet stuffed this place with public art. It's still mostly as it was. The pavilions erected near the children's playground get touring plays, Shakespeare in the park, SuperTed, religion of all sorts, blokes dressed as gypsies, women in robes and bells, jugglers, storytellers by the score. But when the summer ends culture goes. The pavilions get demounted. No installations glint among the bushes; there are no intrusive statues among the leafless trees.

You could swim here, once. But now, like all other public water this stretch harbours virulent algae, stuff that'd take the skin off the small of your back and send you home with testicles swollen like peaches. No move to clean it. The bathing platform and changing rooms have given way to a walkway for fishermen. The water is stocked. The fish have not been asked.

I'm in shorts and walkman. I run, it's a good mile right round. There's something about running next to water, the ozone, the light, the serenity, that makes the straining breath all worth it. There are legions of us. Nikes, track-suit-bottoms, sticks to ward off snapping dogs, headphones playing U2, watches you punch to tell you how many seconds that 1000 meters took, how high the blood count, where the heart is, how to mend it, how the eyes rove out and stick onto glory. Stop and draw in air. Gallons. Climb to the roadside and open the car boot. Find the secreted Malvern and take a long draw. The Lake glistens in the sun or greys and slides in the rain. Either will do. I watch a swan land. He comes in like a flying boat, flick of water, whoosh of air, then a glide to serenity. Calm. That's what the lake is for.

Expulsion of Evil in a Material Vehicle
Roath Park Lake

after dark
steal a boat
pack it with rice, fruit, fowl, two eggs,
beer, insects that ravage the fields
bad syntax scrawled on scraps

fit it with
oars (already), rudder (wood scrap),
sails (pray for them)

scatter bark laden with the sins and
misfortunes that well from our hearts

name it, bastard, untie, cast adrift
point at the five Roath Lake islands
push, hope
see these poets sitting on the midnight
banks, hands to their cheeks blowing

if it lands we are cleansed
if it returns, or sinks, or swamps, or
casts its content to the four winds
then we are once again what we
were before we started
bust

damned
stuffed

(put these words
 onto bark scrap,
 cast adrift on fire,
 just to be sure).

Done by Jan Leslie in 1967
just before destroying an entire
edition of *second aeon*[6] because
it besmirched the memory of Christ.[7]

The leys intersect on these islands without names

The pieces of small mag float out
across Lleici damp.

LAMBIES

Probably the least known area of Cardiff, to Cardiffians anyway, are
the flatlands that lie along the coast, filling the ten miles or so
between the city and Newport to the east. The plain between the
meandering, sink-mud, stinking mouths of the Rhymney and the
Usk belongs to the sea gods and not to us. Most of it is on or below
sea level and is protected from the tides by a continuous sea wall that
goes back to Roman times. The levels are known collectively as
Wentloog, *Y Waunllwch* in Welsh, but Cardiff slang names the whole
stretch after the Lamby Moor, a salt-marsh, quagmire slopped into
the east side of the Rhymney. Fishermen once moored their boats
here, dragged up onto the rucked banks. It was a four mile walk along
the causeway to town and the market. Trade was slow.

The flatlands have a character alien to mountainous Wales. Only
their northern distance rises; east and west roll without incline; south
is the dirty sea. People from such landscapes traditionally do not
cling to each other. Hamlets are few. Lone backwood hunter-gather-
ers, ditch slinkers, opportunists. In the histories of the city the
Lambies hardly feature. Down the centuries these lands have been
home to fishermen, hermits, bear baiters, magicians, sin eaters. The
light tells you. It is bright when the city hangs in drizzle fog. It strikes

in from the south with no hills to hold it, and only sea storms to cloud its beaming face.

Today these tide fields are largely reclaimed although one should use that term with caution. The mire is drained. The landscape is riddled with ground pipes, ditches, reens, channels, trenches, flush cuts, sluices, culverts, sea-gates, pump-stations, ponds, and fields full of runnels, surface gleam, splash and glint. There are few roads. Those there are have water along their edges. Step off and you sink. Hard surface is illusory. The real earth is yards below. The main interceptor sewer taking waste from the Rhymney and Western Valleys comes through here. Cased in 3.5Km HepSpun concrete, the pipes run through the rock below the pastureland, twenty-two meters down.

Taking a research trip we drove east, over rutted track, to the farms that dot the land behind the sea wall. Maerdy, Newton Willows, Lower Newton, Chapman's, Sluice. Between the wrecked, moss-clouded white fronts of the traditional farm houses stand bungalows of orange brick and Mediterranean pantile. Every one has a dog or a horse's head on its gatepost. The land is not used much for crop or cattle. The professions here are horse, dog kennel, scrap metal, turf. The green wet fields sprout so swiftly and the clods of grass come away without effort in your hands. The sea wall south of Maerdy Farm is being raised. Huge earth movers push sludge strengthened with hard core into ever higher dykes. The world's rising waters threaten here as much as they do in Kiribati. The drained land our side of the water sinks. Like a sponge with the damp pulled from it, it gets ever smaller, lower. Less than sea-level. Welsh Netherlands. Just beyond the car dismantler's is a badly hand-painted sign reading BEWARE OF LOW FLYING AIRCRAFT. Half a mile on, skid-crashed in a turf field is a buckled Cessna, rotors bent, no undercarriage. It's been here for a while. There's an Alsatian sniffing its tail fin. Bits of turf are stuck to its paint scratched belly.

In 1606, year of the Great Flood, when half of St Mary's graveyard in central Cardiff got washed down the Taf, the sea wall here was breached. At Peterstone, the now abandoned church has a mark some five feet up its side showing the water's extent. The Roman Peterstone Great Wharf was hastily rebuilt higher and with a path on top. The views from this mud vantage, a dozen feet above the flatlands, are extensive. We slug west along it towards the glittering city. Seaward the Wharf faces a mess of flotsam: old fridges, parts of cars, tree trunks, trashed kitchen fitments, grass and bog. This landscape is broken at intervals by ancient groynes, a cure for coastal erosion, their bust teeth stretching out deep into the Bristol Channel. Drifting out from the scattered farms comes tinned pop, hip-hop, but softly, this is Sunday. In the distance a man exercises a dog. There's no roaring of the unlicensed on bikes, the wet land wouldn't support them. There are no drills nor hammers. Trains on the main line rattle but it's a distant sound. The gulls swoop over the Lamby Way waste dump, a white itch. Take a breath, you can tell something isn't pure, not quite right. Plastic waste sticks on fences, along the reen edges, in the reeds. This is no wilderness. On the foreshore there's a wrecked bike and half a wardrobe. Out to sea is a dredger and a container ship. Beyond them Somerset. Flat. Fenland. More of it, moving south.

The drainage ditches have names – Rhosog Fach, Rhosog Fawr, Greenlane Reen, Blackwater, Towick, Sealan. A keen developer has turned a mess of them into standing pond, stocked it with trout and surrounded it with wood strutted walkways. Fisherman's heaven. But mostly they slink between fields, disguise themselves as reed filled ditches, flow almost imperceptibly. The great reen beyond Peterstone, largest by far, is where, if you believe it, Arthur sailed in with the sword ready for the stone, with Guinevere, with his knights, with his armies ready to smash back Rome. This reen saw those Romans land gold and the Vikings scream in with fire and blade. What you believe depends on who you read. Although there is evidence in some Cardiff place names of Scandinavian origins – Crockherbtown, Wharton, Cathays. But that's also true for large stretches of the UK.

At the Six Bells, much re-built and re-fitted, one of the few pubs along this run of

coast, we get in at the fag end of Sunday lunch. The barman smokes
sullenly. The barmaid, tight top, black Spanish hair, looks like Lara
Croft. On the wall is a box filled with ancient tobacco pipes, bits of
mouthpicces, half-smashed bowls, evidence of the area's human past.
The one family left at table are the far side of a case of wine, charac-
teristically loud with knife-edge Cardiff accents and roaring laughter.
The sun in the west slides below cloud and lights the city red. The sky
itself is bluer than anywhere else in Wales, if that is where we are. Is
this Cardiff?, I ask the barmaid. No. This is Marshfield. She doesn't
know either.

From The Flatlands

12-bell final
Peterstone Wentloog
loose screws
handbells
How to Subscribe
Re: How to Subscribe
Have I missed anything?
Visual Basic peal proving
Constipation from MacDonalds
falseness in peals
falseness in peals
treble jump
falseness in peals
re: falseness in peals
alternative to false peals
re: alternative to falseness in peals
hypocrisy in NATO
falseness in MacDonalds
June newsletter for guild of bellringers
falseness in NATO
re: falseness in NATO
hypocrisy
cylindrical
horse collecting
bell hangers
re: falseness in bellringers

concordia seminary bell
plain Bob triples
falseness
re: falseness
hypocrisy
re: hypocrisy
oh yes
how to unsubscribe

from
The Wentloog Levels
Change Ringers
On-Line Digest

THE PARKS OF ROATH

Coming past Waterloo Gardens in summer mid-evening you can see the attraction. Tight grass, wide beds, paths that snake, unsullied benches. NO CYCLING by all four entrances. This fails to stop kids on fat-tyred two-wheelers from steaming through, breaking the thin lower branches on the park's new cherry trees and frightening the dogs. But it doesn't happen much. This is the park where the silver band plays on Sundays and you take your babies to teach them to walk. There's a brook running through here, looped down from Llanishen Reservoir to the north. It divides into two channels – the old course and, a few yards from that, a dug channel. Joining up the old rivers. Protection against flooding. That happened. There was a tidemark a few feet up the wall of the Dairy. That's a hairdressers now. At the Post Office the stamps almost floated out through the door. NO BATHING warns a sign. And nearby more NO CYCLING. We like notices a lot in the UK. Near here was once the green hut that contained the youthfully carved name of the poet Dannie Abse. He told me where to look but when I visited the hut had been pulled down.

The brook – Nant Fawr, Nant y Lleici – was utterly unpronounceable for the entire length of my childhood. But demographies change. At the back of the Minsters someone's named their house after it. And there's another half-way up Westville. Unwaith eto mae'r Cymru wedi dod.

At night you can stand on the road that separates the Gardens from its larger neighbour, the Mill Park, and hear the piped waters of the stream. Local legend has it that a tributary once sluiced down Penylan

Hill before erupting into the Lleici below in a torrent of meadow flooding foam. But there's little evidence on the old maps. The waters rush deep, now, dark, their magic compromised, contained.

The Mill was real but all that's left is a bunch of worked stones let into the brook embankment. The wheel and its house are long gone. The grind stone smashed. The park here – another in the five mile stretch that arcs from Llanishen to the Harlequin Fields – once grew wheat, barley, oats and beans. Now you come if you want to wreck bushes, throw frisbees or do yourself on drugs. You can hear the young crashing through the weekend dark nights when it doesn't rain. Squirrels, condoms, Castlemain.

As we go north, along the thin Westville Park, dug-up, re-grassed and pathed; shaped like the State of Delaware; the ground rises imperceptibly. Willows weep into the stream by the houses – all different from each other, all with flood marks beneath their hall wallpaper. South of Sandringham Road, running parallel to Westville, was once a brickworks. The clay pits are now sunken gardens. The houses oblivious, industry moved on.

Beyond are the Recreation Grounds. First the bridge, the library, the new community centre, park offices, the bark-surfaced kids play-area with artificial hill and climbing frame like a Frank Lloyd Wright construct. Then the fields – tougher grass – soccer, baseball, running, whooping, dog chasing, things with bats. Rough kids after the war. A downed Messerschmitt. Bust bikes. Bent my arm here once. Now it's cool Asians and Afro-Caribbeans who always score. Top end are the karate mystics, body rings, tattoos, jugglers, and guys with shaved-heads and dogs. Someone with a tai chi sword is slowly slicing through the form, the energy all inside, moving like a man underwater. A pensioner from the rich Ty Draw houses opposite reports him for unsheathing a weapon in a public place. It's my religion, the practitioner claims. The investigating officer replaces his notebook with the same liquid movement the swordsman used. Next time, he says with a half-smile, try singing hymns.

PENGAM

Tracking the Licky I'm along Newport Road with the grit and fume of the four o'clock rush. This is flatland again – Cardiff side of the Rhymney. These acres are recovered from the reen beds, made fit first for brickworks which dug the clay during the city's explosive industrial expansion and later for light industry, panel beating, part assembly, electro plate. Now in the dizzy new century the place is all supermarket, furniture store, car park, drive-in Burger King, pastel glass Castle Bingo. Somewhere here the Licky crossed under, on its way south. There was a medieval bridge, Pont y Rhath, which once carried the coach road. Gone. I looked for arch, pillar, disturbance in the stone walls. Nothing. Not a trace.

The Licky has a history of being moved. Everytime anyone wanted to build near it the course got altered. The most recent episode was in the 1980s when Sainburys acquired what was once the Roath Pottery site for its Colchester Avenue eastern Cardiff enterprise. The new diversion took the brook in metal lined tunnel under the veg and the check-outs, on through cut, culvert and pipe, to flow east instead of south. Of its old track little remains: a wet and overgrown, trash filled ditch dog-legging between Newport Road and the bridge up to the Pengam Freightliner Terminal. The city's new surface grows over its older scars. There are black bin bags in there among the brambles, hard core, trashed out brick and broken plaster, mortar, glass, smashed window frame, buddleia, bramble.

My plan is to find the old airport and to make what I can of the sounds I encounter en-route. Sinclair did this crossing London only he was interested in what he saw – graffiti – meticulously recorded in his spiral-bound jacket-pocket reporter's notebook. Iain Sinclair was born in Cardiff, although that's hard to discern from his writings, the result of thirty years residence in London. *Lights Out For The Territory* is his big city testament. In it, Sinclair, notepad reduced to beer-mat pulp by

the drizzle, records his encounters, follows the spirit lines which link his obsessions, uncovers the City's soul. It's a splendid but silent work. For me, I want to hear what goes on.

Most of the people I pass, a multi-racial stream from the UWIC food college on Colchester or disgorging from further afield by bus, have plugs in their ears that come from mini-disc or MP3. Their soundscapes have no traffic roar or train rattle moving over them. Their east Cardiff runs to a more vibrant backdrop. World as cinema. World, note, not Hollywood. Nitin Sawhney, Ananda Shankar, Vilyat & Bismallah Khan, The Disposable Heroes of Hiphoprisy, Talvin Singh, Bombay the Hard Way, Eminem. I start asking some of them what they're listening to. What's it to you mate? Who you from? You're from the Council you are sod off. A girl with her dark hair stuffed up inside a knitted cap and wearing trainers with soles like moon boots tells me she's got Stevie Wonder. Her thin friend in the long sky-blue coat has Spooks. Life's a time warp. There's an old guy coming down the hill pushing a bike. Cap, grin, bag of leeks hanging from the handlebars. I stop and ask him. He slows, shakes his head, no idea what I mean. Deaf aid. Points a gnarled finger at his ear. Moves on. The 16.00 hours GWR to Paddington does it along the main line. This diesel looks mighty but it's slower than steam.

From the bridge you can look into the freight depot. The trainspotters have websites up showing visitors how to get to this vantage point. Turn Left. Park over the bridge. Up to 6 units may be visible. Get the numbers down. Me and a pigeon at this hour. Bloke in the depot car park drinking tea from a flask. Someone in the distance pissing into the bushes. Neither of them listening to anything but this far away it's hard to be sure.

Go back a century and this bridge led to open moorland – flat and green right down to the sea. Tidefields, swamped at spring time when the fresh water rolling down the Licky and the Rhymney met the grey salt sea water rushing in. In the 1930s McAlpine spruced the sea wall up to ten feet high using Irish labour. The reens were deepened. The land drained. The Tremorfa housing estate began its eastwards creep. This was the site of Pengam Farm and, on its seawards side, Cardiff Municipal Aerodrome. Opened in 1931, this corporation wonder was home to airspeed bi-plane acrobatics, wing walking, wonderful upside-down flying, parachute descents, aerial marksmanship and formation bombing. These were Sir Alan Cobham's *Continuous Programme of Thrills*. The Big Events of The Civic Week. 12 Aircraft. 20 Events. 11.30 am to dusk. Admission 1s 3d. You could you go up as passenger and experience an unprotected five bob loop. The air circus. They drew the crowds. The airport itself was a cramped 176 acres with a short runway. You could fly to Weston-super-Mare from here for 9s 6d. During the war the airport was requisitioned and became RAF Cardiff. It acted as a packing station for Hurricanes, Gladiators and Seafires being sent overseas, mainly to the East. Cambrian Air, unspectacularly serving places like Bournemouth and Torquay, was the last company to fly from here when all operations transferred to Rhoose in 1954.

Where Pengam Road turns to Whitaker Road stands Ellis O'Connell's Secret Station. Twin conical towers full of steam and vibrant significance, markers of Cardiff Bay's Eastern Gateway. These are Bay Art Trust public art installations. New age monuments. Steam pumps out from fissures in their cones. The curved rods which balance on their peaks are wave form railtrack, echoes of the steel which once poured from Cardiff Eastmoors. The muted ore-rust colour of the cones' sides recall the shade the air once was. There's little sound here. Just passing traffic. Wind in the trees. O'Connell comes from Derry in Northern Ireland. Derry rather than Londonderry. Fits the demographic make up of the area in which the sculpture now stands.

Following the raised Rhymney river bank south takes all of twenty minutes. The meanders here are fervent and many. Where the River Authority has installed concrete defences against erosion the glutinous mud glistens. I step in, thinking it'll be no more than an inch or so deep. My trainer sinks to half way up my calf. The slide is palpable. The gloup and woop as I extricate myself take me back to childhood. Soft mud is such a memorable thing. The old airport the river and I pass on our right was taken over in the sixties by Leyland for the assembly of Land Rovers and then knocked flat as, in the face of recession and Japanese innovation, UK car manufacturers sucked their horns right back in. It's called Swallow Fields now. Covered with Beazer and Persimmon Homes, saleable up-market,

neo-Georgian detailing, Brookside driveways, lawn and bushes. Never seen a swallow. Gull maybe. Reen diving duck.

The Rhymney Sailing Club sits on a salient formed by a tighter than usual river meander. Boats high on the grass bank, a long slipway across the polished sink-mud banks to the floating landing stage below. When this river was clean, centuries back, the waters were coracle fished. Wood-post henges from which static nets were hung were rented to locals. Catches were steady. Rawlins White, Cardiff martyr, burned to brilliant God-fearing death for his protestant insistence in 1555, worked at the estuary[8]. No roads then, just swampy tracks. At the Local Studies Library in Cardiff centre I asked to look at the large scale map of this area, drawn at the end of the nineteenth century. On the map table it was two foot by three of whiteness. A thin black line showed the coast, a scratch showed Lower Splott Farm, but there was little else. Just emptiness. No road, no drainage ditches. Marsh, tidal flats.

In the club yard, where a number of the boats look as bad the river mud, someone in old-fashioned brown-orange coveralls is yacht painting a hull. You ever seen any henges out there, I ask. I point down river. He looks blank. You know, posts, tree trunks, they used to hang nets across them. Make a catch. He shakes his head. No. Nothing like that. It's just mud.

When I reach the estuary two boys on push bikes have preceded me. They bowl through marsh and swampy grass utterly fearless. Your bike will go anywhere when you are young. The shoreline is littered with smashed hard-core, clinker, sea rounded brick and polished mortar. There's a burned out Bedford van and a spray of swooping gulls. The land is pooled with free water, tall seed bearing grass sways at the edges. I look back inland, my feet again sinking deeply into the swamp beneath me. I take a photo that avoids the electricity lines and the pylons and manages not to show the yachts at the Boat Club nor the edge of Tesco Extra[9] that's recently opened to serve Beazer's clients. This is how the Cardiff Moors must have been for centuries. Silent, slow. Full of air, rain and standing water. Then a helicopter clatters over and the reverie is gone. I go back to the road, not far, and slog my mud-filled shoes and caked jeans back to civilisation. It's twenty minutes to the rail line. The allotments are full of onions and black earth. Someone is singing Frank Sinatra as they dig. I get out my notebook again and write that down.

TY DRAW

At right angles from the side of Ty Draw Road in Roath – the long road that defines the eastern edge of the Recreation Ground – runs Ty Draw Place. Along with Penylan Place and Linden Avenue it's one of a group of short streets that once filled the gap between the main road and the Roath Dock spur of the TVR, the Taff Vale Railway. This ran through its cutting a couple of hundred yards on up the hill. A pannier tanker pulling thirty wagons of coal used to go through here every half-an-hour. Rattle and hum. The line was built to service Cardiff's Roath Dock which opened in 1888. It rolled from the huge sidings at Mynachdy to the Port marshalling yards. There were sidings too at Newport Road to service the now vanished twin-cooling-tower power station. The line steamed passed allotments, house backs and rough grass banks, until, in 1968, coal finally gave up. Kids played here. Set the grass on fire in dry summers. Put halfpennies on the line to have the engines flatten them into paper-thin harvest moons. Train spotted – 3729, 4123, 5644, 3403 – such magic numbers. Ate liquorish root. Sherbet. Chewed Black Sambos.

There's little left now. The cutting is filled and built upon. Mock Tudor Brookside houses. Hydrangeas, bamboo, fuchsia bushes, roundels of grass, chain-link, and car park spaces which totally obscure your front door. They are overlooked by Wales & the West Housing Association flats: Hillside Court, Redwell Court, Stonewell Court, Oldwell Court. The names of the ancient houses that once stood on this hillside hang on. I lived here. In the terraced bit. Childhood home. The Ty Draw ('The House Over There' in Welsh) headquartered the farm

that once occupied this slice of slanting, soggy meadow. The Parks below were a swamp of reed, stream and drainage ditch. The rains poured off the Penylan hill clay into the Lleici – Roath Brook – the only thing left now to remind us of just how wet this place had originally been.

Going back to look at the house again is odd. Rosemary Strinati with her foaming hair and dark dark eyes no longer

lives next door. There are no boys constantly repairing their black, boxy Austins over the road. The house is narrow and tall. Far narrower than I remember it. Shed out back. Chicken coop taken down. Up to ten of us once lived here – a whole extended family. Two stoves, five fireplaces, coal in scuttles everywhere. No TV. Cowboy books on the shelf. At Christmas the turkey was always too big for the oven. To be cooked it had to be lugged to the bakers off Marlborough Road and then lugged, steaming like a pannier tanker, all the way back.

I ran my first magazine from here. *Dynamite*. George Pitten and I were the only contributors. Football stories, baseball, adventures, stuff about Roy Rogers and Dan Dare, quizzes, lists of American cars. Text dominated. We'd tried cartoons but neither of us could actually draw. I once contributed a list of coal wagon numbers to fill space. The cover usually had something in red exploding on it. Easy to do. No poems. Who'd read them? The magazine only ever had one copy, of course. We couldn't afford printing. It was produced on white quarto paper bought in twenty-five sheet packets from Woolworths. The pale brown packet wrapper served as *Dynamite*'s cover. Pages were never numbered. Binding was not bothered with. We rented the thing out. People dropped it on the floor and scooped the pages back together in random order. An early B.S. Johnson[10]. Penny a read. There were a few takers but never enough to actually cover the cost of the paper. We subsidised the thing by cutting local lawns and running errands for reward. Same principle, really, as for later literary magazines I would edit. Hope. Write loads of it yourself. Shuffle the pages when the binding failed. Put your hand in your pocket to pay the bills.

In the back lanes some of the original gates and garage doors remain. Hanging on rusted hinges, worn and bent. Repainted, but with rotted footings, and original green flaking beneath. I check for penknife carved names, forty year old graffiti, but can't find any. Liaisons happened here. Hip flasks. Illicit bottles. Cigarettes. In the dark, knickers were lost. So I heard. Never saw anything myself.

The Penylan Hill bridge is about all that's left now of the railway. And even here the bridge sign with its ownership name and contact numbers has been stolen. The lane alongside, with typical care and consideration for history, has been renamed Boleyn Walk. Queen of England. Died 1536. Never came here. Nor her husband. For a time the bridge was in use as a road underpass until, abused by dopers and the destitute, it got concreted solid by the council. Steps now descend to a pit[11] where trains once rattled. Standing there it's hard to get the atmosphere. No space, too much grass and infill. No smell of creosote, chunks of charcoal, grey-white stone ballast. Small boys in khaki shorts jotting numbers into notebooks. John Davies with a jumper full of stolen apples. Peter Hughes with his rabbit's foot. John Kachinski with his airgun. Where the line was – piles of leaves. Where the steam was – sky.

Back at Ty Draw Place all is silent. Potted conifers in the front garden of number three. Slabbed over, no grass. Green door. It had one that colour when I was here. There's a cat drowsing on a wall and someone's put a SUMMER FETE notice in their front window. Two white Ford Transits outside. An Audi 80. A Golf. At the top, Boleyn Walk is a highway. Ghost trains roar next to it. Cowboys gallop along its sides. I remember all this. I used to be one of them. Mack over my back like a cloak, bamboo rifle in hand. The past is such a glorious country.

THE LOST WELLS OF PENYLAN

Look beneath the Cardiff surface and you'll find an older, less Christian, more pagan past – the well cult. Water has been holy in these lands for millennia before St David. Its veneration is almost as old as water itself. The gods of springs, sumps, lakes, rivers and wells could heal, make fertile, bring wealth, control the weather, cause the tribe to win in battle. People bowed down before them. They were worshipped. At their abodes were made ceremony and sacrifice; gifts were left; spells were incanted. The druids built their altars near water sources. When Christ arrived the world changed irrevocably, as we know, but a thousand years of pre-Christian custom and belief could hardly be extinguished overnight. The early Church (the Roman Church, remember we're well before the reformation here) took the course of appeasement followed by gradual change. The Papal instruction to St Augustine, one of the earliest of the Christian missionaries, was to hold back on the zeal and convert pagan custom 'into a Christian solemnity', slowly, so they didn't notice it happening, by stealth. The temples, rocks, altars and sacred places were to remain, only the belief was to change. The idols of Britain would be destroyed but their houses would not. The devils and demons would disperse making space for the real godhead to arrive. Jesus of good, of passion, of the water sources. But in these damp, windswept lands of Wales old custom was hard to shift. The well, abode of the oracle and of the curative spirit, would stick hard for the next thousand years.

Holy wells are holy because time has attached reverence to them. They are places where water seeps from the rock, rises from the grass, flows slowly from a niche in some escarpment. A number trickle, some form pools, many flow on as brooks and streams. Some have structures built around them: bowls, worked edge stones, caps, platforms. Many have no more significance in their appearance than a mud puddle after a rain storm. But their power is undoubted. How else have they lasted, working against the social tide, for hundreds of years.

In Penylan, east Cardiff, there were at least three, all with their own ceremonies and specific powers: Ffynnon Bren, Ffynnon Pen-y-Lan and Ffynnon Denis. In Welsh *ffynnon* means *well, fountain*. In the scratchings of local history that have come down to us there are tantalising references to these curative, holy spots. According to the nineteenth-century historian and collector of Cardiff records, John Hobson Matthews, Ffynnon Bren was "a well situate in the garden of a thatched cottage, by the side of Albany Road, opposite the end of Claude Road. In this house Job Richards was born, and it belonged to his father. Job often cleaned out the well himself. There was no masonry about it, but a hedge surrounded it, and approach to the well was over a stile. People came to the well from far and near, with bottles and tins, to carry home the water. They took it, both externally and internally, as a cure for bad eyes. They did not drop pins into the well[12]. His father did all he could to prevent people going to the well, as they fouled it. It was the finest water he ever knew. You might stir up the mud as much as you liked, but in half an hour the well would be as clear as crystal. It never dried up, and never froze. Job has known people come there with pots and pans for water, when they couldn't get it anywhere else. The water of yr hen Ffynnon Bren was like ice in the summer, and like milk in the winter. You could drink so much as you'd like at it."

Ffynnon Pen-y-Lan, the second well, was situated higher on the hill, in the grounds of Ty Gwyn Farm, near the old Well-Field and Bronwydd Houses. It sprang from a rock which had been walled to form a basin. On the lip was a clay bowl six inches in diameter with an impression in the firing like the imprint of Christ's knee[13]. The well was venerated and often found full of bent pins left as offerings from petitioners. Nearby bushes were hung with rags. This is what you did. In place of gold you left a pin, in place of a sacrificed animal you left a fragment of cloth. On Easter Monday there was "a sort of fair"[14] held round it. Dancing, roast pig, small beer, the selling of charms. Men on crumhorns and Thomas Hardy instruments. Coloured ribbons among the dampness. When the farm changed hands in the mid-nineteenth century, William Morgan, the new owner, would have no truck with the well superstition and the consequent trampling of his land. He barred access, although the determined still got through. The Ffynnon Pen-y-Lan told the future, cured ills and administered good fortune. Its ghost, a grey lady in sombre garments (they are always thus), haunted lone visitors. "Hold my waist, pull me tight" she is reputed to have instructed one young man who had gone there to sort his failing lungs. In the dusk he was frightened witless. "Pull tighter," she cried. He did but his grip failed and the ghost soared off screaming, "two hundred years before I shall be free." Watch the spot in around 2050. She'll be back.

The third, Ffynnon Denis, good for scurvy and for fixing bad eyes, was a seep from the ground which formed a pool. It had a ghost too. Another grey lady, another lost soul, wailing for release from her bondage in the depths of the night. This one followed the drovers, imploring them for release. My readings told me that Ffynnon Denis was under Roath Park Lake, its waters welling there before Bute gave this tract of land to the City and the boating lake was formed.

Ffynnon Denis, lost under ducks and the lines of men hunting fish.

Checking the sites of these ancient *ffynnonau* began terrifically well. In Francis Jones's *The Holy Wells of Wales*[15], the only survey ever made, I found a tantalising reference in the gazetteer: "St Denis's Well. In Llanishen parish... in 1905 it was described as a shallow pool inside the northernmost enclosure of Roath Park." Could it be still there? I drove up to look. It was. A dark pool in the middle of the Llandenis Road oval, surrounded by trees and boggy grass, rarely visited. In pouring rain I clambered across. Two ducks in the centre. Clear water, full of dead leaves, traffic cones, old prams. You could see the source slowly bubbling, the excess trickling off to join the Licky brook. I hunted the grass for discarded spectacles but couldn't find any. Obviously Ffynnon Denis had fallen from use.

Trying to find the remains of the other two proved much less successful. Putting old maps over the new, pressing, squinting, and measuring took me to the narrow lane which runs from Albany Road to Wellfield Place. This is the last relic of the old Roath Village, the cottages and houses that once stood in this block have all been knocked flat for a hundred years but the infrastructure of road and pathway remains. The lane was choked with butterfly bush and blowing trash. Where it bent there was a heavy municipal bollard fixed to prevent bikers from burning straight through. No stile, no trace of one. The back gardens were built on with slate grey house extensions dating from the thirties. Scrambling, I looked over the wall. A scrap of back yard. No water. Bush. Grass. Bren bubbles into the sewers under MacDoners, the local kebab shop. The chips are brilliant. The rats below can see for a million miles.

Ffynnon Pen-y-Lan – the prima donna of the Roath well cult, visited by Christ, petitioned for millennia by the limping, the mangled, the weak and the lame, cursed beside, venerated, honoured, sung to, praised and beatified – this wonder could not have gone. Too important, how could it? I tracked it, on a day of bright low sunlight, to the edge of Eastern Avenue, where the cutting for that dual carriage way is crossed by the bridge of Bronwydd Avenue. At the spot where the well had to have stood was a Jewish old people's home. I climbed between bushes, peered over fences, peeked behind walls, looked under bins. The ground was like sponge, the green not yet on the trees. Below me the cars roared their streams of exhaust. Wrinkled faces watched. What was this man in black, muddy shoes and a Rohan anorak doing poking among their wisteria? I smiled. Impassive, unflickering, the regal faces stared back. Nothing. Where was the bowl, where the venerated lip, where the seep and holy flow? Gone. Now the brilliant water trickles underground along a deep flowing sewer. Culverted. It empties below into Roath Park Lake. The fish all know their futures. The swans sing hymns. The whiteness of the Scott Memorial never needs cleaning. The glisten of the water's surface has been there for a long long time.

Text Message
From Ffynnon
Denis

Fnd tp Rth Pk
Lk
a pnd h2o seep
sme bbbls &
1 duck
trfic cne & frdg.
put drp on eye
in
strng drzz
mke sgn of crss
dnt do a thng

Ptr Fnch

notes

1. Arthur Cravan – boxer, eccentric, editor of the review *Maintenant* which he sold from a costermonger's barrow, dadaist, surrealist – went to Mexico in 1918 and was never heard from again.
2. A karate stance.
3. Transported from Bowood in Wiltshire. The porch was designed by Robert Adam.
4. The house was built in 1927. The first owner was Rex Samuel, professor of music. He made no structural changes as far as I can tell.
5. *second aeon*, a literary and poetry magazine of international reputation and, for a small mag, considerable reach, was edited and published by Peter Finch, along with an attendant stream of other books and booklets, between 1966 and 1975.
6. Issue 2. Pink cover, v rare.
7. "Moloch! Moloch! Moloch! the almighty god / I turn to you".
8. White is recorded as occupying five Cardiff henges – Fulford Henge on the Taf, the Nabbs, the Moor Henge, the Ridge Henge (near the western weir) and the Lord's Henge near Pulkye, off Roath – "a place on the Severn shore, east of Splott farm". His knowledge of the scriptures, drawn from the Cranmer Bible, was unequalled and he was given to reciting passages loudly and at length in public. During the Queen Mary Tudor restoration of Catholicism, he was asked to desist and recant but he refused. God was with him. Bishop Kitchen sent him down. He was burned to death at a site near Cardiff prison. A plaque to his memory was erected in the Town Hall but vanished when that building was demolished in 1747. A replacement memorial in bronze was made in 1903 and hung on the wall of Bethany Chapel in St Mary Street. The Chapel now forms part of the interior of Howells department store. The plaque is still visible, among the shirts, in the men's department.

9. When Tesco Extra at Pengam opened in 2001, with bunting, greeters at the doors, razzmatazz, bargains and balloons the travellers encampment, just to its rear, arranged to burn a stack of car tyres and, what looked like but couldn't have been, a pile of dead animals. The black, foul smoke billowed through the posh car park. You coughed into your carrier bags. Cultures met.

10. B.S. Johnson (1933-1973), modernist, poet, author, published his famous novel-in-a-box, *The Unfortunates*, in 1969. Chapters were unbound and could be shuffled in any order.

11. This space, too, is being filled in. The mark of industry on the landscape reduced to memory.

12. Votive offerings of the period. Other objects dropped into holy wells include needles, pebbles, coins, keys and buttons.

13. In Istanbul, at the Topkapi Palace, they have two impressions of Mohammed's foot, taken from the desert. They are venerated as true relics. Why should Christ not have gone this route first? The feet, for those who collect such data, are both right, and both are different sizes. There is no record, now, of the size of Jesus' knee.

14. Transactions of the Cardiff Naturalists Society, 1903.

15. Francis Jones, *The Holy Wells Of Wales*. Published 1954, reprinted by University of Wales Press in 1998, ISBN 0708311458.

CENTRAL

BUTE PARK

The Marquis lived a regal life. For most of the nineteenth century Bute Park was his personal back yard. A vast tract of green space running from Cardiff Castle to Western Avenue and the Cathedral, more acres than a hill farm, tree lined, bounded by the Taf to the west and the Glamorgan Canal in the east. This is a Cardiff version of New York's Central Park, with river added. Same joggers, professionals on lunch breaks, winos, mothers, kids and pensioners. The entrance at the Castle Street end carries a home printed sign which reads IF THESE GATES ARE LOCKED PLEASE DO NOT KNOCK AT THE GATE HOUSE NO KEY. Present-day ownership is beautifully unclear.

Beyond the gatehouse where the excavated outlines of Blackfriars sit low in the turf lies a Gorsedd Circle, mixed from rock and concrete for the 1938 National Eisteddfod. The altar stones have a drunk asleep across them. Three Chinese youths throw a Frisbee. In the bushes are crushed beer cans and the brown broken crumple of a cider flagon. The grass moves on, off and away. This is no town park, this is real space. The ice cream van has a cluster of kids buying 99s and choc encrusted Cornettos. A small black dog yelps and rushes in and out of the bushes. The corporation puts public art here each Cardiff Festival. Woven figures are stranded in the plane trees, stumps are hacked by chain saw to resemble the heads on Easter Island, rocks are painted, a vast carpet off-cut from Allied is rolled out beneath the trees. The druggies lie on it. Culture burns.

The character of Bute Park changes as you move north. Space spreads out. The bushes and trees at the Taf's edge recede. The centre

is vast enough to manage 5000-participant fun runs and great public fairs. The Japanese mounted archers demonstrated here. Samurais firing longbows from galloping horse back. Their tents sold noodles, bonsai and sake at vastly inflated prices. Local Zen Arts hero, Stan Rosenthal, demonstrated the fan as a martial arts weapon. The ghost of Basho hovered over the haiku contest but did not land.

On the east side runs the Dock Feeder dug in the 1830s to keep the new Bute West Dock topped with water and to help flush out sediment A weir was built across the river near Maindy and a channel funnelled through the town to reach the dock just south of Edward England's potato warehouse. Cardiff Bay sludge was a great disincentive to shipping. The cost of constantly digging it clear proved exorbitant. The canal-like feeder became a celebrated one-off killer application. The Taf's waters win again.

The Park here is known as Cooper's Field and has been host to everything down the years from military displays to outdoor cinemas complete with huge plastic-glassed bars selling Heineken, Brains and oblivion. Alcohol has such a different character under the stars.

Further, beyond a lateral cross of ornamental trees, cherries, plums, and weeping birch, is the place where tai chi players allow their energy to move by osmosis from the body to the ground. I've seen one hundred and fifty together playing the short form. Brush the knee, chase tiger, repulse monkey, golden rooster stands on one leg. Their baggy black trousers and flat slippers moving so so slowly across the unresisting turf. Tai chi centres the consciousness, moves the body with such small effort. The eyes stay open; they observe, but they never cling. Swimming without water. These martial artists could break your arm by looking at it but they never do. The dance is so different when you actually participate. Swim with them and you'll enter another land.

Bob S. Thomas was never a tai chi player. He'd squat on the verges here, walked up from Riverside, rolling Old Holborn into Rizla papers, staring into space. Thomas discovered writing in the seventies. Born to a Welsh speaking family in Llanelli he was one of life's ineffectuals. Slow, unable; you could imagine him hoeing Iago Prytherch's mangles in a rocky northern field. His poems were mainly dyslectic mumbles done on a buggered Olivetti. Thomas would rub lighter fluid onto the red and black ribbon just to make it work. Like many others he found security and friendship in the gatherings of amateur poets. The small talk, the imprecision, the smoking. Creative writing became a therapy. One to one communication was rarely a strong point. Instead he tried to write things down.

After several minor pieces about eating meat and potatoes and breathing in and out he came up with a triumph. *Rage.* This was a piece of invective, delivered in the style of Dylan Thomas's outpouring against the dying of the light, successful not for its text but for the way it came to be performed. With care Thomas wrote each word on a separate quarto sheet. He stood, raggy-haired and curl finger-nailed, like Methuselah before an audience of beatniks. After the roaring of each word, the page would be torn from its file, screwed and flung dramatically at his listeners. They were stunned. This was performance poetry three decades early. The applause was rapturous. Over the decades the poem was transcribed through many reams of paper but never formally published.

In later years Thomas would become afraid of this triumph, worried he somehow would be forced into having to repeat it and find himself unable, so from around the mid-80s refused ever to read *Rage* again. Some of his early works he sent out to the magazines under his given name, R.S. Thomas, and naturally received a puzzled but absolute success. His awful poems appeared in quite a number of stapled small mags where the editor didn't know better. The local literary community convinced him, eventually, that this was really verse under false pretences. A Welsh version of William McGonagall he might be but Ronald Stewart Thomas he was certainly not. At the Cardiff Royal Hotel launch in 1993 for the real R.S.'s *Collected Poems* Bob stood in line to get, not a book, but his notepad autographed and told the Reverend in mumbling Welsh that he too was R.S. Thomas. The Reverend listened, smiled and nodded. Bookless, Bob passed on.

Bute Park was anonymous and free. The benches were welcoming. The tai chi soft to watch. Before he died, lost and loveless in 1998, the other R.S. spent much time here.

Beyond Blackweir with its bouncing suspension bridge over the river to Pontcanna and the Ambulance Station where the canal lock keepers cottage once stood, are the cricket pitches and the soccer playing fields. Then the Park roughs up. Thick undergrowth, close tree plantings, pines, rhododendrons, squirrel. The Taf Trail, the cycle way that runs from the Bay to the river's Beacons source, cuts through, tunnelling under fast Western Avenue to the north. The Marquis of Bute rode here. There are still stables on the Pontcanna side. But today it's more likely to be helmeted families on bikes or runners wearing MP3 players and knitted hats. Regularly plans are submitted to build flats here, sports clubs, bars. There are attempts to change use, to make money out of one of the City's greatest assets. So far they've all been resisted. Goodway, we'll set fire to you if ever they are not.

ARCADE

Coming out of Charlie Bristol's nightclub on a September Saturday morning, 7.00 am, I decant myself into slow, old sunlight; once drunk, now not drunk, but through the sound barrier. I had reinvented my life. I'd gone in as a young writer who nobody knew and come out changed. I was still utterly unknown, of course, but there was a significant difference. I'd scored. Up there on the long balcony, above the dowdy Victoriana of the Castle Arcade. Finch the poet now had something real to write about. My fake, junk-filled sub-Kerouac beat ramblings could drop and chinks of the real could storm on in. Was writing like that? I'd got through more of the night than I should have on drink filched from tables, stolen cigarettes and unfresh air. Bristol had been expansive. The band had done bad, loud blues; Cream without skill, notes in the wrong places, hair and headbands. The DJ's soul fanaticism had saved it – *Midnight Hour, Dock of the Bay, Fa La La La La* – no mixes, not arrived yet, still gaps of silence between tracks.

The leys crossed here. The celebrated mainline down from Llandaf Cathedral and the holiness of the north sliced right through the dance floor centre. Lie down, spread-eagled, feel the ripple. Make yourself float. Coming from the west the leys of the standing stones, the cairns and the great Tinkinswood Burial chamber of antique antiquity thrust in their pulsing arms. Where the forces mix, said Bristol, was like the Taf meeting the Ely, the turn of heavy power, soul of the city. He believed that on this spot had once stood a huge henge altar slab, a moon reacher of significant power, proof of the ancient forces. This

was a guidestone for Mars landers, a pre-historic Luna-observatory, a seat of the giants, a timeslip, a gateway, King Arthur's grave, sword hard in the stone. He'd tried to check the history. Made a pest of himself at the library where the maps, naturally, never went back far enough. He tried getting into the floor of the basement below (clothes shop) with an ineffectual pick. He hacked a bit into the damp, tanked floor before the alarm went and the men in blue arrived. Proof remained elusive, fluid, entrancing. He told me about it. I believed. Could that be enough?

At the bus stop the cleaners told each other how they were. Smoked. Me too.

Sitting upstairs, front, good view of the turning castle, I got harangued for hair which crossed my collar, for my desert boots dyed green, for my protest badges, for my fingernails, for my shifty eyes, for how I sat, for the time of the day, but mostly for the ear-ring, one only, left side, which my complainant's daughter would never been seen in, which infected everything about it, which told of my dissolute life, which made her wince when she saw it, swaying, youth, god, what were we, foam, growl, o the world is not right. It isn't, it isn't, madam, no it's not. But it's the one we have. Can you imagine this happening now? People wouldn't dare say a thing to a stranger for fear of abuse. But this isn't now. This was 1965, then.

In a later time Bristol would fall from grace, if grace was ever what he had. His life would tumble, as so many do, through relationship foul-up, inability and bad luck clashing, and the drink and dope washing across the eye band would be the only relief possible. Reality has such a sharp, serrated edge. Drink moves over it like the Lake waterfall, step on step, from the glorious white-water heights, all sun and shouting to the sombre pools and ice-coldness in the dark parklands below. I saw him recently moving through Waterloo Gardens, face lit red, Oxfam jacket, bottle of White Lightning clutched easy. I waved. No response. I watched him head for the Royal Oak and peace.

The Arcade runs from High Street, the northern extension of St Mary Street, to Castle and Duke Streets, facing Cardiff Castle's clean municipal stones. These arcades – the Wyndham, Oxford, Dominion, The Castle, St John's, Royal and others – are billed as a major attraction by those whose tedious job it is to sell Cardiff to visitors. Traffic free, covered. They were largely built during the nineteenth century, many by the innovative Cardiff Arcade Company. What's significant about them is their total lack of chain store domination. The Arcades are the last bastions of the city centre small trader. Victorian and Edwardian shops sell shaver parts, second hand books, old records, surfer clothes, skateboards, specialist shoes, electric trains, antiquarian maps, hip jeans, fancy haircuts, leather, American shakes, martial arts weaponry, Christian cards, health additives, futons, artificial flowers, canvases, oil paints, buttons, dj decks, stationery, oriental knick-knackery and pottery owls. Occasionally Arcade landlords bang the rents up and the independents are forced to restructure or move on. But this is only a flicker in the diverse continuum. Dorothy Perkins, Top Shop, McDonald's and the Nationwide have not yet found it worthwhile to move their chrome and glass on in.

In the Castle Arcade, the epicentre from where Bristol once ran his wonderfully named Connoisseur's Club, the Victoriana has been embellished with restored shop fronts, hanging lanterns, serif bold typefaces and an iron balustraded balcony on top. Up here lurk even smaller businesses, events magazines, music reps, the jazz society, places to get your nails painted, but no longer Bristol's late-nite drinking and diving rock the joint. The entrance was off High Street, through the door and straight up. By the twenty-first century the club had gone forever.

Home across the stumbling recreation ground, churned by footballers, gouged into farm ruts and swamped by south Wales rain. The desert boots never gripped, they leaked and slithered, but always looked so bloody cool. I would write. It was easy to pump out stuff about how the soul was doing, navigating its track through time. In this poetry you could do what you wanted – not a traditional Welsh attribute, where metre was (and still is) absolutely supreme – but 60s city youth hardly cared. What the hell did history mean? Who wanted to be tied back by tradition? The poems were glorious, free-wheeling paeans to dissolution. Much more enjoyable to write than to read. Looking back from 2001 they're mostly crap.

North from the Arcade was rumoured the RSG, the Regional Seat of Government, in the case of atomic attack and the destruction of the infrastructure as we know it. Filing cabinets, tables and buckets of water, buried in concrete deep below the delivery yard back of British Home Stores. Committee of One Hundred, CND's radical splinter, wanted this waste of public money and focus for respectable fears exposed, removed, reused. Activists would meet at Bristol's, drink and plot under the wail of white rhythm and blues, the Yardbirds and the Graham Bond Organisation. Cyril Davis' country-line harmonica doing it to the rhythm of sit down, lie down, protest, protect and survive. Nothing ever happened. There was a badly attended Arcade-blocking sit down where, at a given signal (a hunting horn parp, unbelievably), everyone would lie down like an atomic attack had happened and we were now all dead. I didn't want my cord jacket (mod) marked, so positioned myself near the railway-model shop wall. There were only about twenty of us all together, not enough to block but maybe enough to cause a delay. On the signal everyone sprawled. Shoppers stepped over us. Someone got up, produced a Brownie box camera, took a snap, and then lay down again. After five minutes or so there was another parp and everyone rose, dusted themselves and repaired to the Kardomah. Bristol was with us, wasn't he? Or was he in place, resplendent at the KD, checking us in and telling us that we'd all done very well? The local branch of Committee of One Hundred voted the event an overwhelming expression of the people's will and a huge success. CND didn't mention it at all.

The Arcade is still bomb-free. Although the model shop has now gone and the place in its stead sells surfing clothes. There's someone's tag on the lamppost near the High Street entrance and a couple of winos swaying in the sun. A family go by with a recently purchased hi-tech table lamp strapped to the back of a push chair. There's a journalist with a bag of review copy paperbacks bound for the second-hand bookstore. Read, recycle, retread. This is the future. Walking up the centre of the arcade is a man who looks like he owns it, slightly rumpled, never heard of Jack Kerouac, smoking. Obviously trade.

TAF

Many cities are built around rivers. The Thames through London, the Seine through Paris. Ask the inhabitants and they'll know the whole mythology. The net of lost London waterways – the Tyburn, the Westbourne and the Fleet – drag themselves to outfall through pipes and ditches. They are the lexicon of the city, the life force. In Cardiff the Taf slugs through its Brunel-dug new cut, slightly west of centre, bridged and baubled, and cleaner now than it's been in a century. Yet invisibly. Asking round the city centre shopping malls among a randomly-selected bunch of shoppers, skate-boarders and winos, most of whom thought I was some sort of tourist, I found that less than fifty per cent could actually name the waterway. Some barely remembered that Cardiff even had a river. A bay, yes. Clubs, certainly. But a river? Below consciousness.

There are two Tafs, the second, and lesser, flows to the sea at Dylan Thomas's Laugharne, in Carmarthen. But it's the Cardiff version that has world significance. The Scots are Jocks, the Irish Micks, the Welsh are Tafs, outside the borders that is, never within.

Actually I think it is a myth that Welsh people are named after the once-black industrial waste pipe that flows from the mountains to the sea at Cardiff Bay. 'Taffy was a Welshman, Taffy was a thief..." is in reality an English rendition of the name Dafydd, *David*. "*Dafydd* was a Welshman..." This has nothing to do with rivers, even less with Caerdydd. The town was no more than a slob of huts and a broken castle on the edge of marshland when the word was first coined. According to the Oxford English Dictionary that was 1682.

The river begins up there in the hills. I visited its source once with an HTV team to make a film performing poetry among the mountain tops. I imagined a single spot where the Taf would emerge from the peat bog, a low bubbling, a place from which all the great history would spring. What we actually found was a complete valley end full of damp and trickle. The Taf starts among a mesh of water veins, in a hundred seepings, in a net of rivulets. The cameraman sank slowly under the weight of his equipment. I recited. It began to rain.

By the time it gets to Cardiff the Taf has turned from a stream to a fully-fledged and often dangerously deep, brown-water river. For most of the industrial revolution it washed coal dust and iron waste from Merthyr and the Valleys and dumped it in the sea. Nothing lived here. Dead sheep came down in time of flood. No one fished from its banks. But those days are gone. The twenty-first century has brought a new clarity. Canoeists paddle. I've seen a diving duck where the water sluices through Blackweir. And kids swimming too, among the dumped bikes, abandoned tyres and the gash of plastic flotsam which buoyantly arrives from the river's post-industrial hinterland.

In 1997 the photographer John Davies spent several months recording the aftermath of coal production along the river. He chose to alternate shots of wrecked industry with those of silt. Mud and sludge loom large along the river's track and culminate in vast alluvial flats at its gaping mouth. Past now. The estuary has been barraged and a fresh-water lake created from the combined flows of the Taf and Ely. The mudflats have been bucketed by Dutch dredgers. The silt has slid.

There are pipes under the river bed aerating the fresh water to keep the algae back. Watch for the slow bubbles. You can check Davies shots at *www.daviesphoto.demon.co.uk* – a clear and fitting memorial to how it once was.

Where the river enters the city the remains of its industrial heritage are preserved for middle-class recreation. The Melingriffith Tin Plate Works feeder running from the Taf Weir at Radyr is still there, as is a preserved stretch of the Glamorgan Canal. This is now Forest Farm Nature Reserve: beech thickets, yellow waterlily, pushchair-able pathways, lock-gates, horses in fields. Some reckon that the vowel-stretching Cardiff accent peters out round at this spot. Further north, speech acquires a Valley's tang.

Walking down Taff Embankment towards Clarence Bridge, near the river's mouth, there's strong evidence of city gentrification. The river has a proper walkway and evergreen plantings. The banks are blocked with boulder to stop the flow washing them back. Water taxis ply upriver from Penarth Harbour to the Millennium Stadium. Taf Island, an industrial slum in one of the river's elbows, has been rejoined to the mainland and is being developed as maritime housing. More Mallards Reach. Coots land, duck and dive. I can hear reggae drifting over from Abercynon Street and Taff Terrace. The bushes are already strewn with plastic carriers and lager cans. We are good at building, but can we keep things tidy? No, we can't.

CHARLES STREET

At the Estonian Club in Charles Street Adrian Henri's band were tuning up. A guitar clanged and whined against the arbitrary thumping of Brian Dodson's drums. The stage was big enough to accommodate four but the band numbered six. The audience – cord jean, hush puppy, roll-neck – all smoked furiously. In the tiny ante-room bar among the chintz and soft chairs a fat woman in a peasant dress had been squeezing at a piano accordion while big jowled men in bad suits drank vodka and ignored her. She was drowned out now. "You keep our love hidden – like the nightdress you keep under your pillow – and never wear when I'm there." The voice was clear, fashionably Liverpool accented, and engaging. Henri's fat-arse with the rose embroidered on the left pocket swayed in time behind the microphone. Andy Robert's guitar showered, slid and rang. This was the Liverpool Scene, Henri's band. It was 1968 and poetry was making yet another attempt to take over the world.

The Estonian Club had seen it all, for years. Folk club, jazz club, dope club, dance club. Poetry would be just the same. In a later manifestation the place would become the Montmerence, one of Cardiff's hippest discos, and later again a gay haunt full of hard core and yellow lager before being knocked down when the whole block was redeveloped. It's now an orange-brick office rebuild housing *Career Paths*, the privatised local authority Careers Service. Paul Henry, part-time careers officer and poet works here. The verse connection is solidly maintained.

Charles Street was originally built as a quality residential street in the mid-1800s by Charles Vachell who had made his money as an apothe-cary, an early pharmacist. Substances have haunted the street ever since. By the turn of the century retail had expanded east from High Street to run the length of Crockherbtown (renamed Queen Street in honour of Queen Victoria in 1886). It soon reached Charles Street which began its slow change from residential to commercial. Virtually all the residential houses had gone by the outbreak of WW2. The block now containing the Estonian Club became home to jewellers, tailors and on its south corner a place where remembrance day poppies were cut from gash cloth and stuck to pins.

Adrian Henri's influence as the most bohemian of the trio of Liverpool poets, which included Brian Patten and Roger McGough, was more far reaching than he might have imagined. Henri was not only a poet but a painter too. He wore a dangling plastic heart on his denim shirt pocket. He looked like a tall Toulouse-Lautrec and, in the slipstream of the Beatles, read stuff about schoolgirls, love and freedom and how pop culture was the best thing in the world. No one else had

ever put it quite like that. On the back of his success the *Second Aeon Travelling Circus* (Finch, Geraint Jarman, Heather Jones, Will Aprfitt, Dave Mercer, Geoff Sherlock, Huw Morgan and others) played out of tune poetry, feedback and drums to local youth; hipsters queued at Lears for the latest edition of Penguin Modern Poets; and small poetry magazines flour-ished. Hard to imagine now, as you read any amount of verse

you want on-line, that people, a few, once bought these things, took
them home, and held them with reverent hands.

Henri would return to Charles Street, too. By the mid-seventies the
Welsh Arts Council, in a fit of splendid arts provision, opened its first
bookshop and gallery at no 53. This early Victorian three-storey with
walls that let the rain in and menacing subsidence lasted for almost
two decades as the loved and hated *Oriel*, window on the arts in
Wales. On the ground floor the gallery showed artists who were either
too new or too non-conformist to get hanging space elsewhere. Allen
Jones exhibited his women as furniture, Zandra Rhodes had a fashion
show, Jack Crabtree showed his paintings of miners and the hugely
underrated Ray Howard-Jones displayed her seascapes to tumultuous
applause. Above and below were bookshops. Art and culture were in
the basement where the drains overflowed and men had to be called
in to reseal the covers. On the first floor were the books from Wales
and the huge poetry section which ran from wall to wall. Here Jack
Kerouac rubbed shoulders with R. Williams Parry and William
Carlos Williams battled it out for sales against Gwenallt and Bobi
Jones. Naturally there were book launches, author visits, hot discus-
sion, shoplifting and shed loads of verse.

Adrian Mitchell, George MacBeth, Bob Cobbing, J.P. Donleavy,
Michael Foot, Jackson Mac Low, George Dowden, Margaret
Drabble, R.S. Thomas, Chris Torrance, Glyn Jones, Harri Webb, John
Tripp, Pete Morgan, Edwin Morgan, Dannie Abse, Libby Houston,
Friedrich Durrenmatt, Eugene Ionesco, Henri Chopin, Benjamin
Zephaniah, Roy Fisher, Carol Ann Duffy, Lisa St Aubin de Teran,
Andrew Davies, Wendy Cope, Strand, Andrew Motion, Bill Bissett,
Margaret Atwood, Gillian Clarke, and Derek Walcott all appeared
here. Who else? Adrian Henri. This time without a band, bigger, same
jeans, same rose, same smile and same wonderful voice. Writing.
Reading. Keeping the flag of pop alive. Still looking like Toulouse-
Lautrec.

Going up Charles Street now culture seems to have abandoned it.
The Grassroots bands and disaffected cafe is a pale shadow; the
Cellar beat generation coffee bar now an ash wood and Harry
Holland walled wine bar. No bookshops, no art. Even Ffotogallery
with its formidable minimalism has gone, once sandwiched between
the Church and the run of gay clubs which dominate the street's
eastern side. There are no accordions. Estonia no longer needs us.
There, as in the street itself, regeneration has done its job.

GORSEDD GARDENS

Which Cardiff park gets the most foot traffic? Not Roath Lake, crammed with perambulating citizens any sunny afternoon. Nor vast Bute Park, home to office lunches and timeless drunks. But a much smaller place. North of the New Theatre, across the Taf feeder and before you get to the National Museum's Portland stone edifice, lie Gorsedd Gardens. Three entrances, two paths and some of the best maintained flower beds in the city. These are seen daily by the thousands of workers who track from Queen Street, the station and the car parks, to the National Assembly Government (formerly the bunker-like Welsh Office), the City Hall, the Temple of Peace, the University, the Law Courts and the many other official centres of Wales. Here are statues of Lloyd George, high on his plinth, dripping green as his copper degenerates and John Cory – Coal Owner and Philanthropist – silently facing the bushes and the bustle of traffic rolling, along Boulevard de Nantes, in from the west.

Gorsedd Gardens, established when the new City Hall was opened in 1905 and Cardiff declared a city, has as its focus the sandstone blocks of a druidic circle. The central altar stones, in use as a site for drunken prancing right up until the eighties, are now gone but the ring of red, raggedy sentinels, marked with drill holes from their erection and flaky as the rocks of the Heritage Coast, still stand. They are no antiquarian artefact, however. These stones are nineteenth-century quarryings from the cliffs of Penarth. They were used for real in 1899 when the Eisteddfod visited Cardiff and held its performances in a massive wooden shed erected where City Hall would

later be built. That was the Eisteddfod where the committee threw tradition to the wind and opened a bar on the maes; no poem was found to be good enough to win the chair; and on the last day the pavilion collapsed. The omens had all been bad. The stones were moved when the City Hall foundations were dug and it was agreed that they should become the centrepiece for a new public garden. But when

restored the circle was re-erected in the wrong order. Flankers circled and lead stones lay down. And as any stone circle aficionado will tell you they are not supposed to do that. But who cares now? There's no celebratory plaque. The origins have gone.

In the sixties Tom Jones, the macho rock and roll dynamo from Ponty, played the Cardiff Capitol and underestimating his attraction to the massed screamers ended being chased up Park Place and into the Gorsedd's greenness where he hid himself behind a weeping cherry. Today the place gets taken over as a hippie market everytime the city runs a Big Weekend and puts bands on stage across the civic centre. Recently I bought a tee shirt with a marijuana leaf on its front, a Marrakesh lamp holder at six times the price it would have been in the Moroccan souk and had a map of Wales done in henna on my right bicep. Girls screamed and hurled themselves ecstatically between the trees. There were eight skinheads clutching cans of Castlemaine and in the process of passing out at the foot of the Park Keeper's hut. St John's Ambulance were stationed behind Lloyd George but they didn't move. I could hear Asian Dub Foundation doing it through the trees. In Cardiff it, whatever that is, often happens right here. Last year my friend, who really should know better, tried to buy a £10 deal from a sparkly youth who was at least half her age. It costs twenty these days, darlin, he told her. Instead we bought ourselves flat bitter beer and drank it from plastic pint glasses. After a time the world slows down, and so it should.

HAYES

I'm standing at the Hayes Island Snack Bar with a cheddar and white-loaf sandwich and a mug of pale tea. The snack bar, now in at least its third incarnation, still looks a little like a Barry Island municipal deck chair office. Truth is the present building is mostly sham. It was built originally as a parcel office for the tram service and turned into a one-hatch café when trolley buses took over in the 1950s. At this time the open air fruit and veg market lined the road island and you started work at seven. The café served the blackest tea this side of Pontypridd. Now the city centre has been pedestrianised and this spot is half way along the posh route between Habitat and Howells. The new café has decorative blinds, brightly-lit windows and serves a frailer brew that fits the Coke and Fanta palates of our times.

The Hayes is currently designated as the stub of street that runs between St David's Hall and the top of Caroline. Beyond, where the road bends west into the café quarter opposite the Marriott, the thoroughfare is labelled as Mill Lane. But check the old maps and the whole district is called The Hayes. Bute's surveyor, David Stewart, on his 1824 pen, ink and watercolour map has his Hayes running right down to the bottom of St Mary Street. Like language itself nomenclature shifts with the tides.

In Medieval Cardiff there was much more space between buildings. People had their homes here, their gardens, their courtyards. The streets might have been narrow but the buildings spread themselves out. The Hayes, an old word for hedges, were the town's market garden. Veg, flowers, cabbage, roots, beans, sprouts. Local restaurateurs are now hard at work putting them back. In tubs and containers outside, on the menus within.

At the bottom of the present Hayes, where the Glamorgan Canal used to flow under Waterloo Bridge and turn south west to run alongside the old town wall, The Wellington (originally The Duke of Wellington with noble face on the inn sign, now replaced with a drawing of a long green boot) spreads its outdoor-drinkers plastic chairs across the paving stones. On match days this is a surging sea of red and beer. South lies café quarter, the City's answer to Costa del Sol but with added rain. Kemi's, Las Iguanas, Jumping Jacks, and Latino's – an uninhibited wash of drink and spicy food, waiter served under seaside umbrellas and lowering skies. Yet despite the climate this non-Welsh outdoor life appears to work.

Mill Lane is now wall to wall

food and drink-powered leaping but wasn't always. Twenty years back, before the Marriott Hotel went up, Mill Lane faced the peripatetic Cardiff outdoor veg market, moved here from Hayes Island. Behind it was the infamous rock and blues Moon Club. Middle of the run was The Private Shop, Cardiff's fully-licensed porn emporium. The Frys, legendary purveyors of air-brushed Harrison Marks[1], had their stores in Caroline and Bridge Street – they still do – but this was the real stuff. In The Private Shop were counters of knobbly vibrators, racked videos and floor to ceiling displays of shrink-wrapped continental gynaecology. You could brush up your linguistics here. Magazine captions, such as they were, ran in many languages. The publishers aimed at the widest of markets. French, Italian, Spanish, German. But no Welsh. I asked. No demand.

Today things are much the same. The enterprise is still private. It has screens across window and door and a small sign at its entrance warning that admittance will only be allowed to those over eighteen. In the tiny display case that serves as a window is a single copy of the Macvicar video, the red bleached from its jacket, leaving it, like the shop itself, weak and old.

The Hayes were Webb territory in the eighties. On Saturdays Harri, poet, republican, former naval officer, retired librarian, could regularly be found drifting between the Wyndham Arcade's Welsh language outpost, Siop Y Triban, and the Hayes Island Snack Bar. Harri Webb's poetry ranged from maudlin-laden epistles of exile and retreads of Welsh history to protest song lyrics that had you either falling off your chair laughing or wanting to storm City Hall. The Hennesseys recorded them. Heather Jones sang them on TV. The actor, Ray Smith, recited them from the theatre stage. But somehow Webb failed to capitalise on his rising fame as a people's icon. Maybe he looked too much like Captain Pugwash. Perhaps Cardiff was uncertain of its roots. Maybe Wales wasn't ready yet. Over mugs of tea he told me that he'd decided never to speak English again. "No longer appropriate," he declared, in earnest seriousness. "Dim point, ti wel. Get me a bag of crisps, will you?" *Sing for Wales or shut your trap – all the rest's a load of crap.*[2] Harri Webb died in 1994. He was born in Swansea and spent his last years in Cwmdare. Hardly a Cardiffian but, like so many others, attracted here by the lights.

Despite their pedestrianised appearance both The Hayes and Mill Lane are still open to traffic. Taxis, trucks. The café quarter has a railing separating it from the roadway. Small boys can be seen sitting in the Mexican restaurant section throwing chips under the tyres of passing artics. Samba music drifts across the tables. On a hot afternoon, on those rare times we get one, this could well be Barcelona. Not grey blitzed Cardiff. Certainly not Wales.

HIGH STREET

I'm in Cardiff's High Street outside the re-located Oriel Bookshop. The Stationary Office Oriel Bookshop. Before its reinvention as a Business and Professional specialist I used to run this place. We did Wales. We did the Celtic countries. The minorities prospered on our shelves. What language did our customers speak? The game was to spot which that would be before they opened their mouths. Initially this was a tough call. Like most of us here in this Cardiff-based Irish-English-Welsh whirlpool, my sense of identity is blurred. In 1801 the local population was 1,870 with at least half speaking Welsh. By 2001 that had grown to almost 300,000 – mostly immigrants from beyond the borders – Irish, west country, the north, overseas. The percentage speaking Cymraeg had shrunk to single figures. The mix was thick. Does it really matter who you once were?

Spotting the Scots Gaels was simple – they came in as natural caricatures – tweed, socks, sensible brogues. The Irish had the beards, the bonhomie, and the look of rovers. But the Welsh – that was harder. Something about the shape of the face, something about the clothes.

It was so easy to be confounded by black mothers who'd gone to Welsh classes for the sake of their bi-lingually schooled children. Simple to be perplexed by middle-class English managers mid-way through their *Wlpans*[3], in to buy fat Welsh dictionaries or black-bound Bibles that would look good on their office shelves. Learning to identify a Gog (*gogledd*, Welsh for *north*) often ended up being a matter of the shape of the nose.

In the north, where the immigrants rarely go, it's another country.

At least four hours of hill and green desert from Cardiff. Those who live there are geographically isolated, suspicious of outsiders, and resent what they see as interference from the wayward south. In Gwynedd the use of Welsh in some places is as high as 80%. In the south east, where to money is and where most of the population have followed, that proportion sinks to 5%. Nonetheless, over 10% of all of Wales's Welsh speakers – 40,000 – live within twenty-five kilometres of the city. That's a sizeable number.

But is Cardiff a Welsh city? Many like to think so and suggest that it's much more of one than it actually is. Politically that's a good thing. Wales is different. Being another country helps trade and grant aid. Having a real identity in these days of a politically correct much-confused England is something to relish quietly.

Demand for education through the medium of Welsh has risen steadily for thirty years. Sales of things that mark us for what we are – CYM stickers for cars, dragon flags, WRU tops, CDs by the Manics and the Stereophonics, learn-in-a-day language courses – all go well. Cardiff TV aerials are shifting from their gape at the Mendips where the news comes from Bristol to the Glamorgan Vale where the programmes are ours.

That Cardiff does not feel like other parts of Wales should come as no surprise. Paris is unlike the rest of France. Moscow is not Russia. But there are Welsher seeming conurbations: Swansea and Aberystwyth for a start. Cardiff is more anonymous than either of those places. It teems with people who do not know each other, who live mobile lives, who have lost the sense of allegiance which might have held them years ago. The place rushes. In Swansea people talk on street corners. That doesn't happen here.

The perception has always been that if you dig back through Cardiff far enough you'll uncover the city's Welsh original, a place so Brythonically definite that its identity would pose no argument: *Heol y Frenhines* the street signs would say. There'd be no *Queen Street* hanging around to compromise the position. I've subscribed to this idea too, proud of my Welsh Cardiff origins. So I've dug. But I have to say that when I got back as far as I could go under the layers of Norman French and the dark ages that went before them all I found were Romans. Two thousand years ago there were a few fishermen here, certainly, but hardly anything else. The city grew because outsiders arrived and caused it to. Check the old street names. Wharton, Soudrey, Broad Street, Frog Lane, Crockherbtown, Adamsdown. Dim llawer o gymraeg yna. Cardiff centre, the old town inside the walls, the small cluster of streets running south from the Castle have inevitably been the territory of the incomer. The family historians, who assiduously record these things have produced list upon list of the names on record of Cardiffians, going back as far as such records go. The balance is in favour of names which are not native.

What this tells us, of course, is that those in positions of power came from beyond the borders. The local Welsh were working-class, below the need to have their names written down. Most lived outside the old town, in the small villages of Crokerton, Roath, Lisvane, Canton, Whitchurch and Ely. Places that were absolutely and indisputably Welsh, as their street names testify. Crwys Mawr, Dwy Erw Syr Hari, Pwll y Wenol, Pen Heol Llewelyn Maerwr. All places now subsumed by the growing city.

So how Welsh does this city feel? More now than it used to. You can hear the language on the streets, if you listen hard enough. All public buildings acknowledge its existence through uneasy (and often garbled) bi-lingual sign-boarding. Public figures making speeches usually try some stuttering Cymraeg before breaking into silver English. Rather than trust the language we use symbols to mark our identity. The dragon is everywhere: Dragon Tyres, Dragon TV Repair, Dragon Driving School, Dragon Computers, Dragon Financial Services, Dragon Burgers, Dragon Dust Busters, Dragon Hair Dressers, Dragon Massage. Front of t-shirts. On the sides of the buses. Top of the city hall.

Yet this is mostly a form of elective identity. People are choosing to be Welsh, no matter what their actual origins. And that's fine. You may not speak the language much beyond bore da but that doesn't automatically make you English. Your parents may have spoken Welsh to each other but English to you. Your forefathers might have come from Galway or from Somerset, a long time ago. Things are different now. The 20,000 or so Welsh speakers living in the city have no greater claim. They've moved here from elsewhere in Wales, chasing work, taking middle-class jobs in government, in education, in the media.

Cardiff the place that elected to be Welsh. The name of the city clinches it. *Cardiff. Caerdydd.* What sort of Welsh name for a place is that? Caerdydd, as a written form, does not appear anywhere much before the sixteenth century. In the earliest examples *Cardiff* is given as *Cayrtif* or *Cairdyf*. Why not *Caerdâf* or *Caerdav* as in *Llandâf*? Caer means fort. Cardiff fort on the Taf. Plausible, but when you think about it, full of holes. I'm not convinced. Swansea is, in Welsh, *Abertawe*, mouth of the river Tawe, indisputably Welsh. *Caerdydd* sounds made up.

This is a match day. Wales vs. England. The streets are full of youths draped in the flag and the Stadium, new and brilliant, lies just round the corner. A huge capacity covered sports arena right in the centre of the city. Why build on an easy to manage greenfield site when you can do it in a city centre. The Millennium Stadium at the Arms Park. A Welsh first.

If anything pulls us together it's rugby. The Assembly, agreed on by barely half of those voting, should have unified us politically but, by default, the polarisation has continued. In the pub the other week a Scots prat from Aberdeen told me that he thought being Welsh was almost the same as being English. Only a gossamer distinguished us. The deepest insult available. I should have thrown my beer over him or threatened to torch his holiday cottage. But I merely suggested that he should take care with his views and changed the subject. Am I getting soft or is it the culture? On Oriel's window it says *Llyfrau Lywodraeth*[4] in front of a stack of Hansard and copies of the Parliamentary Acts which still emanate from Westminster. The fans are eight deep trying to get into the Goat Major. I stand in line.

In Cardiff, High Street is about as old as you can get. It starts at the Castle, where the High Corner house once stood, and runs south to where the river, before it was shifted west, used to wash away the houses. Here High Street becomes St Mary Street. The junction with Church Street, site of the old Gild Hall. But ask Cardiffians where the two streets join and they won't know. The whole thing is known colloquially as St Mary Street. Only the businessmen, the traders, the planners and the map makers stick to the given names. High Street was once the real commercial centre. The south end of it held the town cross and the great stone where meets were made, curses spat and on which deals were struck. The best businesses located here. Stationers, jewellers, hat makers, furriers. But today the money has moved east to the newer shopping malls St David's, Capitol, Queen's. High Street is downgraded – in commercial terms it's now a secondary location. Pizza shops, Gamers' requisites, outsize outfitters, boutiques. The pub, the Goat Major, renamed after the Welch Regiment's mascot, started life two years before the battle of Waterloo as the Blue Bell. For many glorious years this was an unreconstructed, wood, smoke and Brains tavern. High ceiling, echo, best beer this side of Germany. But now, as we inch slowly towards the brightly lit pumps and my glasses mist with the heat of sweating bodies, it's more like Friday night at the students union. I ask the guy in front of me, check shirt, four rings in each ear, fag, sweat and steam, why he's come here. Brains. What other answer. After the coal this is Cardiff's gift. Strong. Bitter. Dark. Get it down.

Real Names
For Cardiffians

Archer
Baker
Bassett
Beavan
Boucher
Bren
Broun
Brewer
Chapman
Clerke
Collines
Cox
David
Davies
De Raath
Edwards
Evans
Ffletcher
Gawler
Glasscott
Green
Gwillim
Herbert
Hodge
Howell
Humberstone
James
John
Jones
Kemeys
Le Gildere

Lewis
Llewellin
Lougher
Luly
Mathew
Merik
Minnitt
Morgan
Mower
Price
Roberts
Roos
Slake
Steeman
Stradling
Strickland
Sueet
Tanner
Thomas
Treharne
Turberville
Vaughan
Vyner
Want
Wastell
Watkin
Wells
William
Yeoman
Zidrake

Names
from the
Cardiff rolls
sixteenth to
eighteenth
century

(suspect
Zidrake
as poetic
licence)

KARDOMAH

Billy's coming out of the KD fast with half a kilo of Moroccan Red making a bulge the size of a bible in his inside pocket. He could shift, easy, but there's a face at the far end he doesn't like. Safer in the street.

The KD's got old ladies in fox furs downstairs and mods up. Parkas. Hoods. Students. Youth.

The guy with the Italian bush shirt comes in bearing a copy of Adrian Mitchell's "*Peace is Milk ... War is Acid*", printed as a folded handbill by *Peace News*, sold cheap, in the style, exactly, of the penny ballads centuries before. You read the poem. The hairs on the back of your neck stand up.

They won't have war. These people will stop it. Girl in the yellow jeans. The ponytail. The Stones haircut. The beard. The round-collared jacket. The one using the Rizla. The one with the bag from C&As.

Coffee arrives in the national consciousness like a post-war automobile, desirable, shining. The stuff gives the heart a hit into overdrive. But when you're young you don't notice. Not at all.

At the front, overlooking the street, the fifth form are trying it with no money, have one tea between six and eagerness like a rainstorm. Can cope with poetry, the bomb and the Beatles. All at the same time.

This'll all slide apart when commerce demolishes the walls and inflates Timothy Whites from small sensible next door into a vast plc Boots, grown enormously beyond pharmacy, spread from the KD delivery lane to Frederick Street and beyond. But that's not yet.

The guy with the guitar in the soft case can't play. Mouth matchstick. War Resistors International broken rifle in his right lapel. Sports coat doubling as hipness. Has read *Howl* twice. Looking for angels now.

Queen Street outside full of cars and choke. The stunning space of pedestrianisation, when it comes, shocking the city into wondering how ever had they let the past be like it was.

This used to be Crockerton Street until Queen Victoria's Golden Jubilee in 1887. The KD was a slum of veg sold from pots, stink and bad drainage. Sludge. Sailors with sticks. Normans with swords.

By the time the bomb had migrated to missile and the ban had seeped like damp across the West the young had become older and no longer cared. Upstairs at the back of Boots they put in a coffee shop. Crowds get in there. Mothers. Bags. Loyalty cards. Pushchairs with golf-trolley wheels. Cake. Café Latte. Town centre suburbia. No smoke. No Russian Tea.

Dope elsewhere. New dope. Fast dope. Anywhere. Everywhere. A hedonistic Cardiffian nightlife essential. Take it. Do it. Suck it. Blow. No cultural trappings. Not one. Not any more.

THE PARK HOTEL

On the right hand corner of Queen Street and Park Place stands the Park Hotel, three-hundred seater banqueting hall, two-hundred and sixty beds, three restaurants, no gym, four-star, now renamed the Cardiff Thistle and part of a greater empire. It stands opposite the incongruous matching of the Stakis Casino and Gregg's bread and sandwich shop. This is city centre, slap bang. The original Cardiff, of course, never stretched this far. Park Place, or the lane that preceded it, was well outside the town walls. But places grow.

Two hundred years back when Park Place was Dobbinpits Lane the only inebriated around here were the fishermen staggering to market, the wrong side of half a bottle of gin, bearing a string of mackerel dragged from the Taf. The Daubinpits, to which the blind lane led, were the clay deposits where the University Humanities Building now stands. Medieval Cardiffians would dig the wet dirt from here to daub on the sides of their wattle houses. Today daub comes in bags at B&Q and drunks are legion. Park Place is a nexus of clubs, bars and brushed aluminium lager joints. The pedestrianised end adjoining Queen Street runs thick, most nights, with plastered youth, shirt-sleeved alcopop, cider-fuelled and prancing in Dorothy Perkins minimal lycra. The bouncers are wired and wear calf-length black and single gold ear-rings. They look the part. They've seen the films. The red-brick Institute of Engineers on the corner of Greyfriars is now restyled as Creation, ash-floor, neon, Grolsch, couple of basket-weave chairs, an attempt at nacho and salsa dip whatever but mostly hip-hop, thrum and screaming. Side of the queue to get in here one Friday, 10.00 pm, no charge for women, two of them in white scatter-sequined skirts, cwtched against a City cast-iron, crest-embossed waste bin urinating. Shrieking friends like cats across the pavement, full view of the black-garbed guards outside the Scrum Bar. What you lookin at? Laughter. Done with a shake and into the Dylans mêlée. Beats waiting in line.

Much earlier the corner site, where the Park now stands, was the house of John Bradley, postmaster, innkeeper, owner of the great Cardiff Arms Hotel opposite the Castle, mail contractor, and former jockey brought to Cardiff to ride and win at the racecourse on the Heath. This out of town business dynamo had the Dobbinpits renamed Bradley Lane and, following a life-long interest in theatricals, leased his attic to local amateur players. By 1827 they'd outgrown the Bradley attic and our man had joined a consortium to finance their new home, the Theatre Royal, erected on ground at the foot of his garden. The Royal could seat a thousand and for the time looked eminently professional yet appears to have been thrown-up rather than built. Its orchestra pit was level with the road and, given Cardiff's inclination to dampness, regularly filled with water. Players slept on straw slung into the auditorium's corners. Things improved when the Bute West Dock feeder was excavated. On its route south the conduit passed to the east of the Royal and drainage significantly improved.

In the theatre success never runs indefinitely. In 1877 a dropped cigar reduced the building to ashes. It was rebuilt as the Theatre Royal mark two, in Wood Street, later to become the Prince of Wales (theatre, then sex cinema, finally amusement arcade) and, more recently, as a further extension of the city's alcohol provision, the first of Cardiff's many vast and music-free Wetherspoons. The derelict Park Place site was purchased by James Howell, draper, white-goods purveyor, and haute couture merchant, who formed a consortium to build the gothic splendour that forms the present hotel. Commercial travellers selling to Howells Department Store

were advised that orders might be larger if they booked into the new Park rather than one of its cheaper rivals. Howells further developed the site to include the Park Vaults bar, restaurants, a ball room and the vast Park Hall Theatre. The UCI concept of combining film with food, drink and leisure is no twentieth century American invention. Wales got here first. The Park Hall could seat an amazing 2,500. It offered entertainment for all choirs: Kandt's Brass Band, Shakespeare, Mrs Annie Besant, theosophist, speaking on 'Reasonableness and Reincarnation', music hall monologues. When the live stage lost its edge the place became a cinema, pioneering surround screen CinemaScope. Yet eventually, with the rise and rise of television, it failed. Its site is now half Thistle conference hall and half hotel car park. CinemaScope, or something like it, you can get on your room's wide-screen TV, if you want.

The Thistle front bar is decorated in French Empire style. Prints of ancient vases embellish the walls. The tannoy plays discreet Mozart. The draped velvet curtains keep back the drunken scream-ing from outside. There are free newspapers and, depending on how bothered the bar staff are, complimentary nuts and crisps. The place is a calm, aged oasis in the centre of a adolescent vodka-powered storm. It stays that way by hiking its booze prices and banning guests from entering still bearing flame-grilled quarter pounders from Burger King down the road. The US rugby squad, billeting here for the World Cup and ignorant of convention, carried on as they did at home. Feet on tables. Strewn across the antique seating, sockless, in day-glo track suits. Their empty fries containers were tidied by frowning waiters. No one said a thing.

The Park's atmosphere changes according to its guest list. It's on the north Wales coach trail and often features Cymry from Bala or Bangor, bedecked in terylene, clutching their sherries and their glasses of wine. The gogledd Bryn Terfyl fan-club filled the place to capacity for the night of his concert at the New. The swaying cardi-gans began sedately enough, impressed by the Park's cod-sophistication but soon abandoning city slickness in favour of hearth-fired choral favourites. A piano was demanded. A piano was carried in. The St David's Hall Barber-shop Singers Contest and Convention attracted a hotel-full of beer drunk, tough females in quintets, dressed alike, Docs, red tops, striped jackets, slogans across their backs, hats, uniformed like cheerleaders, pom-poms, badges. They argued but didn't sing. All of them smoked. The Isle of Man Pensioners Celtic Society, all sixty-eight of them, uniformly turned their chairs towards the bar for an illustrated lecture on local history. Their bony blonde leader spoke in fluid tones of Cardiff's Norman conversion and of Ifor Petit's sullen, unwarranted attack on the Castle. When I marched to the bar for a pint of Kilkenny, the only mock-Celtic beer on offer (and later taken off as unprofitable), a fearsome be-ringed dragon in the front row, arthritic knuckles, tweed poncho, and complete with aluminium, hospital-issue stick shushed me vehemently. I took no notice.

But it's still an oasis. In the decade or so I've used it I have only ever failed to get served once. That was during a Liberal Party Convention. The bar was a sea of yellow, smoke and sweat spreading out through the double-doors, into the lobby and on up the stairs. I went next door to the glass-fronted Scrum Bar for a bottle of pale. What's that, asked the barman. At least that's what I think he mouthed. I had on a jacket. Among the swaying strapless tops and short-sleeves I was totally overdressed. I left and walked up the former Dobbinpits, passed William Burges's Victorian Gothic Lord Mayor's town house at no. 20, now a nightclub, more shirts, more shrieking, passed the Reardon Smith Lecture Theatre, the shipping line's gift to the city. Passed the Student's Union, the University, the Gym, the Registry Office and kept going until I'd crossed the railway and reached the Woodville. Cathays suburban normality. Inside the place was solid with students singing Calon Lan. I couldn't see the bar. Back at Southminster there was a six pack in the fridge. I went on home.

THE PEARL

If you look at John Speed's 1610 maps of Cardiff you'll see a walled town hugging a meandering river. To the east and west are great marshes open to marauding floods and tides. To the north the disenfranchised Cymry; southwards the still clean waters of the Bristol Channel, and the open sea. At the bottom end of town is the great church of St Mary. Cardiff is tiny – fifteen or so streets, a castle and two monasteries. These, flanking the battlements, one to west and one to the east, are the poor and holy houses of the Black and the Grey Friars. In medieval times Christ was still strong.

Today both monasteries are gone, long gone. You can walk the foundations of the

Dominican Priory, Blackfriars, at the Castle end of Bute Park. The walls were largely collapsed by the late 1500s and it was the Marquis of Bute who rediscovered the foundations when he was creating his great park in the mid-nineteenth century. Greyfriars, to the east, stayed the course for much longer. After the Dissolution the buildings there were turned into a town house by John Herbert and used by his family for two centuries until internecine dispute, decay and inevitable collapse set in. In terms of local history they were long lived. The walls, or some of them, were still standing as late as the 1960s; a seven hundred year monument to how the city had once been. Developers, however, have no heart, no soul, no sense of the past. Why should they? Money is a matter for today.

When Pearl Assurance House, Cardiff's first genuine high-rise, was built on the Greyfriars site in 1967 the builders arrived wearing white contagion suits and carrying oxygen. The JCBs had uncovered mass grave pits from the time of Black Death. The Plague could still be there, waiting its chance, still alive in the ancient bones. But there was nothing to fear. Cardiff's damp had seen the evil off. The trenches went in, the dust and debris came out. Llywelyn Bren, leader of the Welsh revolt of 1315 and whose wooden tomb was here when Rice Merrick visited in 1578, was excavated with the rest. Lost. Glass and concrete were all that was important now.

At twenty-six stories the Pearl was high. Given over to offices with terrific views – the Welsh Development Agency and the Crown Prosecution Service both relished their sea vistas – the building had lights on top to warn passing aircraft and became a marker for Cardiffians everywhere. You could see it from Bristol, from the Vale,

from far out to sea. At Christmas they put an illuminated star on top. Yet as a structure the building was hated. Inappropriate. Ugly. Damaging. Unwelcoming. Inessential. Uncalled for. Unwanted. Built despite. In your face. You're having it. Screw you.

Around its base were multi-storey car parks for residents and a large expanse of paved court. Sky buildings require space in which to flex themselves where they touch ground. Over the years there have been a million bright ideas for the use of this pedestrian bonus. Excellent, many of them. Make it a cafe quarter, put out tables, chairs, sun umbrellas. Let it out for open-air art. Paint the slabs. Run a market. Kids' play ground. Make music here. The ideas arrive from the mouths of out-of-town developers, wizz kids, impresarios with an eye to demography and foot traffic. Never from those who live and work on Greyfriars and who know well that the tall Pearl pulls down wind and spins hurricanes where once the sun simply shone. From the bookshop that for a time occupied a ground story here shoplifters were regularly seen losing their prizes as the gusts shook their coats from them and blew their lifted paperbacks away like leaves. The space ended as an irregular spin for skateboarders and a place where drunks tried to lie down, but found they couldn't.

In our literature the Pearl is one of the least mentioned of Cardiff landmarks. In the flurry of novels and short fiction with a Cardiff background that have appeared in the last thirty years no-one appears to have plotted the high-rise in. Duncan Bush, John Williams, Dannie Abse, Lewis Davies and Sion Eirian give the block scant coverage. Great writers, however, regularly visited, read-at and launched their works in the Oriel Bookshop second incarnation, which took over the ground-floor premises when it moved here from Charles Street in the mid-nineties. It sold lit, crit, po and fic until the space was rebuilt as sparkly Ha-Ha's bar and eatery in 1999. Literature flourished against the sounds of ducted air conditioning, slashing rain and distant car alarms.

In 1998 the building changed hands and was rechristened Capital Tower, a name almost all locals have decided to ignore. The incoming venture capitalist developers have reclad the car parks and re-hashed entrances and walkways to bring the Pearl into the Twenty-first. The bookshop, galleries and job centre which occupied the lower levels during the '80s and '90s have been replaced by wood-laminated, silver café-bars where the food looks like art work and is served on oversized plates by slim black-clad waitresses with towels folded neatly into the backs of their belts. The money flows from the pockets of the new-gen young. Their target of regular alcoholic oblivion differs only in the matter of scale from that of the gin palace and skunky pub clientele who were here before them, centuries ago.

On my most recent visit I sat in Ha-Has with a Heineken and a plate of multi-plex sandwiches and felt utterly dislocated. In a former incarnation I sold poetry from this very spot. Hard to imagine. Then I noticed the woman at the next table had a copy of *The World's Wife* in her bag. Carol Ann Duffy. The acceptable face but still the real stuff. The world still on track.

Lifting

Chew string. Make it as wet as you can. Lay it along the gutter of your chosen book Put it next to the printed plate you wish to remove. Replace the book on the shelf. Leave quiet for five minutes to enable the saliva to penetrate the paper. Return and slide the plate out. It will detach soundlessly. All art should be free.

Wear a greatcoat. Large, scarf, double breasted, flap and hang. Books can slide in easily from shelves at waist height.

Bags. Never underestimate the two handled tote, open zip, half full of compressible clothes. Drop in the paperbacks. Crush them down.

Fall over, diversion. Accomplice clears the shelf.

Fall over, diversion. The stock you shower from the shelf with you ends up under your coat.

Fall over, diversion. The books you have in your briefcase they help you carry to the door.

Insult the counter staff. They will not want to continue eye contact. Help yourself.

Take the book to the cash point and insist it's yours, given to you as a present in error, you have it anyway, you don't want it, it's a mistake, can you have a refund, this once, no receipt sorry, you are a regular customer, say so, even if you are not, smile, yes yes, smile again, they flicker, the money waveringly comes at you, take it and go.

Remove the £80 art coffee-table masterwork from the display

shelf and boldly march with it out through the entrance. Such audacity. Half the time no one will notice you've gone.

Complain. Makes you innocent.

Run. You are usually faster.

Not at closing time or first customer. Join the crowds mid-morning, lunch-time, 3.00pm Saturday afternoon.

Oh the brilliance of the Christmas run up and heavy rain.

Oriel prosecuted. The manager could manage 6 minute miles. He could then. Someone once made off with 400 postcards showing the grave of Dylan Thomas. Oriel got them all back.

STADIUM

From the hills look south across Cardiff and the chances are your eyes will light on one of two ubiquitous structures. The older is the white, churchlike building that was once Spillers flour mill, glorious on the flats of the Port. The other is the gleaming, four towered ufo, landed like a visitor from Andromeda, crouched by the sleek, silver Taf. This second is, of course, the largest retractable-roof public structure in Western Europe, home of rock as much as rugby, the Wales Millennium Stadium. What do we think of this place? Do we like it being there? We do. Do we love it? We do. We do not.

The Stadium is built on the drained, reclaimed land revealed when Brunel realigned the Taf to the west in the mid 1800s. This damp parkland ran from a big house built facing the Castle. This was the Cardiff Arms Hotel, erected on the site of the Red House Inn which had been destroyed by fire in 1770. Bute stayed here, rather than at his Burges refurbished Castle. The beds were softer. And there was beer. The Cardiff Arms was demolished in 1878 when Castle Street was widened. The Angel Inn, next door, remains. Its original façade can be seen next to the Castle Arcade. The park, the Cardiff Arms Park, given by Bute to the Town, with the caveat that it remain for recreational use, became, in 1848 the first home of Cardiff Cricket Club. As interest in spectator sport increased among the burgeoning industrial-age Cardiff population cricket was joined by football and, in 1874, by rugby. The

Wanderers played the Glamorgan 2nd XV. History began. Crowds arrived. Stands went up. The open space, the parkland, became fenced. Charges were levied to walk on Bute's munificence. A focus for Welsh nationhood started to grow. The river flowed.

On a Sunday in 1997 with most of the Arms Park south stand gone and men in hard-hats racing the clock with their tools of demolition the auctioneer begins the bidding. I'm here by accident, walked in from sunny Westgate Street, chasing the fuss. The old Arms Park is being knocked flat to make space for the lottery-funded great white hope, the Millennium Stadium. The memorabilia has to be worth something. The man with the hat and the tannoy is turning it to cash. The content of the changing rooms, the boxes and the bars have already gone. He's taking bids for the seats. There's a crowd of fifty or so. Sunday best: trainers, sweats, jeans, slacks, family groups, hot dogs, cans, valley voices. Someone wants Row G seat 45. That's his. He sat there for thirty years. He's going to get this for his sixtieth. She bids. She wins. She gets G45 and six hard polypropylene red fold-ups either side. Take them home today in the back of a pick-up. A bluff fifty-year old in a loud check has bought himself twenty-five to put up in the garden round his barbeque. Doesn't matter which twenty-five, so long as they come from here. Local clubs bid for lots of fifty to re-erect in their own tin-shack, wood and roofing-felt stands.

The pitch causes the greatest blood rush. It's being sliced and sold. You can actually buy squares of green sward, the hallowed turf from the holy ground. The bids mount as Welsh clubs battle for their own slivers of green luck, to be trimmed and relayed with care in the centres of their own boot pocked grounds. Someone gets a piece that will go into the middle of his front lawn. Another wins enough to relay a tennis court. Wrong sport but who cares. The magic will travel. This is grail, this is. Glory runs in its wake.

The new Stadium opens in 1999. Wrangled contracts and bad blood brought it in on cost. Laing, the builders, lost a fortune. The four corner masts that hold the vast sliding roof in perfect steel-heavy suspension gleam white above the City skyline. The Empire Pool and an array of other surrounding landmarks have gone to make space. The pitch runs north-south rather than east-west. The turf comes on pallets. You can take it up, store it in a shed near Bridgend, use the space for shows. There's a wooden walkway suspended over one side of the Taf. Neil Jenkins runs on and uses his unerring boot to break the world points record. The crowd of 72,500 scream like they're not going to stop.

On the tour, WRU insignia gleaming, our guide is built like a forward. He's wearing inconspicuous Docs, hard and heavy, good when you are on your feet all day. His line in jokes is soft and easy. He's left his flies undone. Among the twenty-one Germans and twenty assorted locals in our party no one is willing to let him know. We tour the Away teams changing rooms, suspended floors, individual baths in a communal enclosure. Larger than life cuts-outs of the Welsh team stand around for dramatic effect. The tannoy plays a Graham Henry before-game inspiration psyche-up. Punters get snapped standing next to Neil. This is still the Arms Park, our guide tells us, the Wales Millennium Stadium is merely at the Arms Park. When the Millennium Commission's three-year contractual stipulation is over the name will be auctioned. Highest wins. This could well become the Mitsubishi Nippon Arena at the Arms Park. Or the I Don't Believe It's Not Butter Stadium. WRU needs the sponsorship. He smiles. The Germans make notes. Someone takes a photo of the bar staff loading a dozen barrels of lager into the 42-person capacity lift. We move on.

In the open air Harriet the hawk is circling to frighten off the seagulls. There's a crowd-roar tape playing for atmosphere. The kids in the party get a chance to have their photos done holding a replica Rugby World Cup in the Royal Box. I go up the ninety-six steps to the stadium top. Looking back down gets the vertigo flowing. Try chucking an empty can down from here. Wouldn't reach. Brilliant, says the man next to me, a pensioner wearing a red Welsh team shirt. Different every week. Rugby. Soccer. Pop music. Boxing. Wouldn't like to live here. Bloody noise. On match days the city centre becomes one vast, swirling party. Middle-aged men with painted faces. Kids in fancy dress. Women screaming drunk. Brings the trade. Most of Westgate Street is already wall-to-wall drinkery. Wood and glitter. Omnipresent plastic glasses. People pissed everywhere. Don't bring your car in. Don't use the station. Don't walk St Mary and certainly don't try to check the history of Quay or Womanby. Good for business. Makes Cardiff the true international centre of our country. A World-class venue in the city with more hotel beds than the rest of Wales put together. We relish the fame but not the effect. For many of us love will be a long time coming.

THE GENERAL

The main Cardiff rail station, British Rail's grand Cardiff General, has the words *Great Western Railway* cut large in the Portland stone portico, high above the main entrance. Under privatisation it has been renamed *Cardiff Central*. It spills passengers in from London, from Swansea and Carmarthen, from Crewe, and from the south Wales valleys directly into the windy sprawl of the main bus station. On a good day, in steady rain, the mix of destitutes, winos, kids on dope, red-faced vagrants and tattooed, tin-whistled, be-dogged *Big Issue* sellers could not make a better entrée. Thank you, mate, have a nice day. Right here, where transport, toilet, burger house and porno-rich news-stand meet, Wales raises its flag. Croeso i Gymru. During the Rugby World Cup a fire-breathing dragon was erected on the roof of what used to be big Asteys, on the bus station's far side. Fans clustered on the pavement beneath it bearing brown pints. The City run their council-tax rebate and rent assistance offices from a showroom next to the taxi rank. The multi-storeys rise like bone racks. This is not a glorious place.

Unlike the Taf Vale Railway terminus, now Queen Street Station on the other side of the city, the General was built to serve more than one rail provider. Brunel put it there when he drove his broad gauge[5] steam line in from Gloucester in the early nineteenth century. The town burgers had convinced him to re-align the Taf further west and to bridge it, taking his line on to Swansea. The pat of land revealed was drained, filled and established as a main rail intersection serving the new Great Western, the Barry Railway, the Rhymney and the Taf Vale.

The land to the north, where the bus station, Hyper-Value and the Western Mail and Echo Thomson House print plant and offices now stand was leased by the teetotal, god-fearing Jacob Matthewson. He built Temperance Town, a development of cheap, afford-able workers housing. No pubs, much rising damp. Wood Street, named after Colonel Wood, the land owner, bisected the original estate. Rail visitors to mercurially expanding Victorian Cardiff were greeted by gaggles of the poor, their smell and their tawdry house fronts. There were beggars and pan-handlers. There were no drains. In the Cardiff rain the earth-topped streets turned readily to brown slush. For a time this was how we lived. However, Temperance Town didn't last, although some of its atmosphere seems still to be around.

The present day answer to the problem of what you see when you arrive is to turn the whole station round. Cardiff Central will face south, towards the Bay and the glories of our new development. Visitors will exit under the tracks and emerge in a brilliantly lit new plaza where fountains play and inner-city, evergreen plantings soften the concrete. This is Callaghan Square, public art, bike racks, disabled-friendly, lamps, and the re-sited statue of the third Marquis (Cardiff's famous *Monument*) already in place. It's a great plan although most arrivers still appear to be exiting to the north.

On the station's platforms the trainspotters in anoraks remain. The slow transition from steam to diesel, from speed to sloth, from pride to pusillanimity has not altered the affection these data gatherers endlessly have for transport on rails. Carriage numbers are as good as those which once identified the metal engines of fire and steam. Their single-minded obsessiveness is legend. Nine straight hours in drizzle, half a pork pie and three new sets of Valley Line diesel cars to add to the collection mark up a great day. For a brief period in my former career as a bookseller I had a boss who was a real fan of trains. He commuted to work each day from the west country and had a set of numbers attached to the front of his London desk. These showed just how many rail miles he'd travelled that year as well as how many hours he'd sat aboard. He had a statistician's brain and compiled stratas of data on timetable accuracy, coach seating density, and the speed at which his transports moved. His stats were processed on an Amstrad PCW. Their continuous stationery print-outs filled cupboards. And, oh yes, he collected train and carriage numbers. He did that too.

Once, at a Cardiff board meeting with the Quango from whom he wished to make a professional acquisition, he

was in mid-presentation when a train rattled past outside. The offices
were alongside the Rhymney Valley line where two-car diesel sets
were a staple. Our man faltered momentarily, took pen and pad from
an inside pocket and then rushed to the window to take the numbers
down. He was quick. It was over in a matter of moments. Before the
assembled bureaucrats had time to realise what was happening our
man had resumed his discourse. We can offer you a lot, he said, Data
is important to us. We record everything that happens. The bureaucrats nodded. The deal went through.

At Cardiff General the ghosts of steam fade as the ductile,
sonorous, brushed aluminium of twenty-first century living arrive.
The public art works have bits of poetry on them. The unloved brick
pyramid on the station forecourt is embellished, arbitrarily, with the
words of Waldo, Catherine Fisher, Idris Davies, Douglas Houston,
Gwyneth Lewis, Emyr Lewis and others. They read like an enthusi-
ast's haystack, chosen because the artist liked them, jumbled in a
sprawl. *Cardiff* gets a mention once. "No sooner than I'd arrived the
other Cardiff had gone" Dannie Abse. The coffee shop sells latte,
individual green apples, and blueberry muffins. On the newstand
there are more computer titles than newspapers, two books about
railways and a wall display of Lewis Davies' splendid south Wales
novel, *Work, Sex and Rugby*. Two men with briefcases and shiny shoes
are speaking to each other on cell phones. They are at opposite ends
of the booking hall. The whirl of city arrivals passes between them.
This is the centre, after all.

Star Class

*from the Ian Allen Combined Volume, the trainspotter's bible, mostly past now, the steam
shrieking Star Class are all scrap metal, the fictional half-cone boiler of 2001 is yet to be
built*

North Star
Dog Star
Evening Star
Lode Star
Lone Star
Rain Star
Welsh Star
Rip Star[6]

Rock Star
Red Star
Wet Star
Rough Star
Crop Star
Seren Dwr Cymru
Lovely Royal Wales
Sunglasses
Pants

In his youth
John Ashbery
Spotted trains.

But he never
Came here.

THE ROMAN FORT

If we hadn't had the bad mud to the south of us and the insurgent
Silures camped in the woods above Castell Coch to the north then
things might have been very different. Cardiff is hardly a Roman
town. Not on the Caerleon model – no bath houses, amphitheatres,
temples, just a few extant stone structures, hardly any historical
tourists. But the invaders did come here. Cardiff was a staging post
on the main east-west route along the coastal plain. The Via Julia
Maritima – the Roman road – was paved, edged, straight as a Roman
die (which is a bit wobbly but straight enough). It rolled in from
Caerwent, arriving between Penylan and Llanedeyrn, to sweep along
the line of Newport Road and Queen Street to the great Fort in the
centre of town. Not that there really was a town at this stage. Cardiff
before the Romans was no more than a place where you could beach
your fishing boat with a shepherds' hut or two sinking in the mud
near the banks of the ever-meandering Taf.

Via Julia Maritima, the Julian Maritime Way, named after the General, Julius Frontinus, ran from Gloucester to Neath. His Cardiff Fort was a vast thing, at least twice the size of the current Castle, extending out beyond the present walls as far as the Queen Street shops. This wooden structure was a *vexillation fort*, built to accommodate part of a legion. It was the first of four such structures, with later constructs being made of stone, each built on top of each other over the ensuing four centuries. Stone and mud bank, beaten courtyards, stone passages, guarded gateways. The Romans had steam baths, running water, and heated rooms which did not fill with smoke. The contrast between how they lived and how we did at the time could not have been greater. But the Roman mark on Cardiff has been slight. There's the villa in Ely: a few grass bumps, delineated by park benches. Fragments of the Roman road north have been unearthed near Blackweir. And at the Fort there's a 230 yard stretch of the original wall visible in a covered gallery. The Normans, who developed the site six centuries later, flung their edifice up using Roman footings, Roman stones, and where they still stood, actual sections of Roman walls. The bits that are left can be seen outlined in red sandstone, crumbled and poorly mortared, extensively on the south aspect and again on the east and on the north.

Cardiffians mostly ignore the Castle. It's a civic enterprise, Ddraig Goch and Union Jack together on top, structure repaired and polished. It's used by Lord Lieutenants for ceremonials no one cares about and no one understands. In the late seventies I went round with Philip Donleavy, Council Leader, a man keen to make art a real part of our culture. He took me through, showed me his excellent, commissioned Harry Hollands and the awful fifty yard-long wall moulding which darkly replayed a mash of history in the long gallery, facing the Roman wall. Art matters, Alderman Donleavy told me, people must be allowed access. For a moment I was almost convinced. But the economics are always against us. Entrance through the gate to the clipped green and the strutting peacocks was, and still is, more expensive than a casual local caller is willing to bear.

After Magnus Maximus left in 383 little is known of the fort, or indeed of Cardiff itself, until William the Conqueror's large ditched motte surmounted with a wooden keep went up in 1081. Robert Fitzhamon, the first Norman Lord in these parts and enemy of local chief, Iestyn ap Gwrgan, made the wood stone and rebuilt the outer walls. It's been more or less downhill ever since. Welsh insurgency. Success. Defeat. Skirmish. Rebellion. Fire and brimstone. Hangings. Quarterings. The traitor's death and dragging through the streets of Llywelyn Bren by the Despensers in 1317. The Owain Glyndwr reprisals two hundred years on. In the seventeenth century the Castle swayed between first the Royalists and then the Parliamentarians. It shone for a bit. Then the rain fell for decades. And the walls decayed.

By the time of the Seven Years War with France the Castle had become a military prison. When Napoleon made threats it became an army training camp. Between panics the gentry squatted. By the end of the seventeenth century it was again a roofless crumble.

In the eighteenth century the Bute Family inherited. The first Marquis engaged Capability Brown to landscape the grounds. The second Marquis did some minor roof repair. But it was the third Marquis, the enterprising dock builder and maker of the modern city, who turned the Castle round. He brought in the architect and fabulist William Burges and created, from what was still essentially a Norman war outpost, the extravagant High Victorian fantasy we see now. Burgess installed Gothic spires, golden stalactites, carved four-posters, Chaucerian insignia, Biblical wall paintings, a clock tower, a roof garden, fountains, and gold-encrusted Moorish ceilings. Fairyland appeared in the middle of smoke-thick Victorian Cardiff.

This could have been a nineteenth century Disneyland if the Marquis had been letting the public in. But he wasn't.

The famous animal wall, carved stone sea-lions, lynx, pelicans, sea-horses, monkeys and lions, was erected along the Castle's front. The lions had to be recarved because in their first incarnation the Marquis thought they looked too tame, too much like pets. He wanted roaring. I'm not sure that's quite what he got. Following mid-twentieth century street widening the wall was moved to its current location on the Castle's west side. Mervyn Baldwin restored the stonework in the eighties. At night these frozen beasts, with fresh noses and new ears, prowl the devious, dangerous city. Check Gillian Clarke's Animal Wall poem. It's all there.

The contemporary Castle gets rented for weddings and banquets. The tour, which includes sight of two strutting peacocks, an amble through the Welch Regimental Museum and a look at what the 1st Queens Dragoon Guards have left, costs an arm and a leg. In the fifties I promised half my classmates at Marlborough Road Junior School that I'd meet them outside the Castle when the millennium turned. The world might totally change, we imagined, but the Castle would not. On the great day I went to Ifor Thomas's party where we drank ourselves stupid, attached poems to rockets and sent them to burn in the sky. Outside the Castle some dusty memories might have showed, dark amid the fireworks, but I have my doubts.

Pink Floyd played here when they opened Chapter Arts Centre somewhere around 1970. Tom Jones leered and gyrated like Frankie Vaughan on dope in 2001. The battlements are adorned with flags, banners, and hangings. At night light projectors turn the stone to liquid. Neon streamers zig-zag along the sides. The castle shape has to be obliterated. It is history. A Norman, invader, conqueror, oppressor's past. Castle – this is the symbol of everything we now aspire not to be. The world has moved on. The English now settled here are Welsh. Most of them. Or, at least, they say there are. The bright lights shine, especially in the Bay. Square foot for square foot Clwb[7], in Womanby, attracts more people daily than the Castle ever can. That's a victory of sorts, pale but just palpable.

WOMANBY

Coming up Womanby Street in an August afternoon with the sun on my back. There are three women in front of me wearing heels that haven't been this high since 1961. They've got glittery bags big enough to hold a cigarette lighter and a lipstick. One's got celtic inter-lacing tattooed around her bicep and the other two have ankle chains. I've no idea if they are going out or returning home. This is the oldest part of the city, the dirtiest, the most exciting.

At one time Womanby would have risen away from the town quay at lower Westgate Street. Before the Taf was realigned, tall ships unloaded their cargoes more or less where Macdonald's and the multi-story car park are now. The Glamorgan County Council Staff Club would have been a sailor's tavern. The Millennium Stadium a tidal swamp. Womanby, the name is actually a corruption of *Houndemanneby,* a Norse word meaning 'huntsman's dwelling' or something like that, goes back to the twelfth century which is possibly an all-comers record for Cardiff. As a thoroughfare it is narrow and dark, readily betraying its medieval origins.

As the street rises slowly past the City Arms, an unreconstructed Brains pub now taken over by youth, Jones Court appears on the right. This tiny run of nineteenth-century workers terraced houses are the joy of the local council. Restored to chocolate-box perfection and with the most beautiful of pointing they are cleaner today than they have ever been. They are home to an architectural practise and the council weights and measures department. There's a gate that locks the quiet Court from night-lively Womanby. Dope deals are done in its shadows.

Beyond here, where the old town slaughterhouse once stood, is an anonymous building into which the girls I have been following turn. They vanish through a boarded door next to a notice which announces rebuilding. There'll be another club open on this spot soon. There are a bunch of tourists here in soft shoes and plaid pants taking photographs of each other with the Castle at the top of the street as a background. Cardiff Marketing are at last seeing some results from their work.

For its size – it's only a short stubby little thing – Womanby has a huge number of drinking places. It always did have. Westgate Street's vast Wetherspoons, The Gatekeeper, has a rear entrance here. Above The Horse and Groom (which was once called the Red Cow) is the goth and thrash metal Blue Moon. Opposite is the famous Clwb Ifor Bach. Established in the 70s, Clwb was a bright new intrusion for traditional Cardiff drinkers, most of whom had either west country or Irish origins. To get in not only did you have to join but you also had to siarad cymraeg. Economic necessity, however, eventually forced the owners to relax this rule a bit at weekends. For their part most Cardiffians had no idea who Ifor was. They imagined, perhaps, that Mr Bach was the owner. An entrepreneur down from Blaenau Ffestiniog. Here to make a buck from his fellow countrymen stranded in a heathen, English-ridden southern land.

Ifor was actually a Glamorgan chief whose base was in the trees above Castell Coch, on the hills which surround Cardiff to the north. In 1158 the Norman, Robert Fitzhamon, ensconced in Cardiff Castle, decided to have done with the liberty and privilege of Hywel Da and to impose new English law on the local Welsh. Ifor Bach, the little and very strong, would have none of it. He raided the Castle, scaled the walls, and kidnapped Fitzhamon, holding him and his family until the imposition was revoked. The Normans always found the native Welsh hard to control. Periodic upsurges against authority have formed the basis of our way of life ever since.

Before it rose to fame as Clwb Ifor, the Womanby Street four-storey premises were home to the British Legion, doubling as the Middle Eight Jazz Club at weekends. Control was tight. Punters arriving for an evening of local big band music were handed cyclostyled warnings against using marijuana. Beer was okay. Weed was not. But on most nights that sweet smell was still there. Same thing today. Champion Jack Dupree[7], the black boxer boogie pianist with the diamond stud in his ear, played the Middle Eight in the early sixties. It was the blues boom and the place was packed to the entrance stairs. Dupree, who at the time lived in Paris and was hardly the downhome cotton picker his listeners expected, hammed the part. He leered, winked and smarmed black music at an almost entirely white audience. The place began to lose its feel of Queen and Country. This was the blues, man. Yes. Right here. Right now. Dupree got included in rounds. People gave him cigarettes. The piano top became stacked with pints. The good times rolled. At precisely 10.30 a badge and blazered Legion official came on stage to tell us that o dear o dear the licence wouldn't allow it and we had to stop. Dupree smiled, sparkled, and boogied seamlessly into Mama Don't Allow No Piano Playing Round Here. A cheer went up. The house continued to rock.

Top of Womanby, three or four dark doorways on, is Dempseys, Bia Agus Deoch, the Irish reincarnation of Brain's Four Bars jazz pub. Facing the Castle and as disreputable as it can be while still staying open, Dempseys is where the drama students go to test their one-acters, bikers to beat their brains flat with alcohol and black dressed goths and weirdos to smoke their mostly paper rollups and sip at their halves of beer. The Cardiff literary scene flows in and out of here like the tide. *Cabaret 246*, the eighties performance poetry workshop risen from the ashes of Chris Torrance's university creative writing class, met in a back room, weekly, for years. *Undercover Writers*, the less mouthy extension of that idea followed on in the nineties. Antony Howell tested out sonnets concerning his mother's bodily function, Tôpher Mills reinvented roofing as a vehicle for genuine poetry and Chris Broadribb retrod Allen Fisher before changing his name to Ozzard and fleeing west.

Benjamin Heath Malkin, traveller, coming past the end of Womanby Street in 1803, was not that impressed with this slice of ancient city. The Welsh consider this "a neat and agreeable place", he records but he found it had little "symmetry in the construction of its buildings" and was not much pleased with the accommodation or the layout either. Mud and waste. Awkward corners. Little new paint. Things have been really slow to shift.

LOST RIVERS OF CARDIFF

Can you lose a river? When I began looking into the past of Cardiff I imagined that rivers would be the constants. Water moving from hill to estuary, in trickle and in flood. This would be the structure onto which I could build my history. As it turned out nothing could have

been further from the truth. To start with rivers meander. Given free reign, unhampered by hardcore embankments, artificial weirs and cut channels, they vacillate like vipers. Most of Cardiff, that part south of the line from Penhill to Penylan, is an alluvial plain made up of sediment and sludge left there by the area's three principal rivers – the Rhymney, the Taf, and the Ely. These are called the Rempney,

the Tam or the Tib and the Eley in the earliest records. Across these Cardiff moors the rivers snake and unsnake themselves as flood, tide and whim demand. To try to understand them I laid out my maps of their estuaries, drawn over the last six hundred years, on top of each other. The river mouths, showing up through the paper, seemed to dance. Mud elided, tide fields greened then fell, the mouths actually moved. From one map to the next they did not stay in the same place. As rivers meander so they bend into S shape. The bottom rim of that shape becomes eroded by the water's flow. And as its edge moves southwards, towards the sea, it trails the thrash of the river in its wake. A live thing, always shifting. These moors, these flatlands of marsh, mud sink and water-course, rifted with reens and thick with swamp are a Welsh Bangladesh.

When habitation arrived, the early Cardiffians proved unwilling to let things remain as they were. Advantage had to be taken from that which God had given. Quays were built. Channels were cut through estuary mud enabling ships to navigate the huge tidal fall, fifty feet, second largest in the world. Rivers, where they proved difficult, were realigned. The most dramatic example was the straightening of the errant Taf *during* the mid nineteenth century. This mighty Welsh mud thumper – a pale brown paper tiger in summer but try it at a spring flood – once bent in towards the town, south of Cardiff Bridge[9], to wash along the west bank of St Mary Street. Quay Street ran from High Street like a slipway directly to the wharf. If you'd looked between St Mary Street's buildings and you would have seen the masts of ships. But it was never a happy arrangement. Regularly the overfed Taf would flood basements, wash away housing, and, on one spectacular occasion, the whole graveyard and half the walls of the original St Mary's Church. Check the station side of the former Prince of Wales Theatre. High on the wall more or less above the mobile flower seller can be seen the church's outline. Not real but memorial. Yet this *is* where it once stood. In 1851 Brunel was brought in to engineer the *new cut*, moving the river west, to run across the

Great Park, freeing the town, until the arrival of the barrage, from the threat of sea water in its cellars.

The Taf, however, is hardly a lost river. It is still very much with us, cleaner now it no longer has to carry the iron, coal and waste down from fifty miles of wretchedly hard-working valleys. Industry has deserted Wales. Its two hundred year excitement is over. The river is clean. Effluent runs in pipes, not in surface watercourses. Throw a coin off Canton Bridge and you'll see it arc in to lie there on the pristine river bottom. Well, not quite. But almost.

What *is* a lost river is the Tan. This mill leat sluiced from beyond Blackweir predates the arrival of Bute. It slithered in from the north, across the damp flats that are now Bute Park, to seep toward the Castle, feed the moat, run the Town's twin mills by the West Gate, and then eventually deposit itself in the Taf which it entered just below the Old Quay. Speed's map of 1610 shows it, along with a set of fellow travellers, sliding south under the towns walls. West Street went over it using a small stone bridge situated just beyond the Castle. Known also as the Tanyard Brook this slow trickle of a watercourse took the waste from the tannery which, until 1861, stood by the old West Gate of the Town, Taf side of the Castle. A Burges replica of that gate is still there. The effluent – animal parts, dye, offal, carcass fluid – acceptable in the medieval period when humans simply topped the mess with waste matter of their own – became less so as the Industrial nineteenth century took hold.

Jonathan Swift, looking at The Fleet, one of London's many lost rivers, saw how quickly a rainstorm could turn a trickling seep into an unacceptable torrent of foulness, carrying with it a rage of waste:

> Sweepings from Butchers Stalls, Dung, Guts and Blood,
> Drown'd Puppies, stinking sprats, all drench'd in Mud,
> Dead cats and turnip-tops come tumbling down the flood.

The Tan stream went under. With the mills gone and the tannery replaced in 1858, the Town Surveyor was ordered to draw up a plan for the "passing of the Tanyard Brook into the Town sewers". Land drainage and the new West Bute Dock Feeder had taken much of the water from source. What was left was culverted and now flows through the sewers, deep below the Cardiff Arms (later The Angel) Hotel. There's a thirty foot Roman well here too. Hermetically sealed. Does the manager know what moves beneath the feet of his dignified, well shod guests? The water they drink is blue-bottled Malvern from the

Worcester Hills. Below flows the native product, unpalatable, but real.

Herbert Williams, the poet and historian, was asked to leave the bar here once for not wearing a tie. Not that he was drinking water, red wine was better. I was with him. I had no tie on either. We wanted to discuss creativity, the new poetry that was now ripping through Wales, the history that got us here and the glorious future. Herbert was into railways, stagecoaches, love, lust and the things that actually made Wales work. The manager, like a good Roman, was dignified but firm. Much movement of the hands but no actual pushing. Down the steps and into Westgate Street. Off you go boys. We went.

Nant-y-Ty-Gwyn the Whitehouse Brook has also completely vanished. This stream rose in Llandaf Fields, towards Penhill, and tracked its way, west of Cathedral Road, along what is now King's Road, to cross Canton Common, and eventually hit the Taf where Brook Street now is, in Riverside. When they are declared to be in the wrong place town streams appear to follow a common pattern of degradation. As water gets drawn off for industrial or residential purposes their flow becomes reduced. Paved streets and house drains leave less rain to reach them. If you cover the land's surface with buildings and then metal the roads the rain and water simply does not sink in. Lost rivers reduce from stream to brook to trickle, from a flow crossed by bridges to a ditch crossed by planks. Dark ditch. Black ditch. Dumped in. Overgrown. The Whitehouse Brook, also known as the Canna, (and the Turton according to some sources), was never actually an all-powerful watercourse. It was a mild thing. It had one tributary, the Glas, a stone bridge across its north end, Pont Canna[10]. That was lost to sight when the top of Cathedral Road was developed in the late nineteenth century. The Whitehouse ditch was condemned as a 'nuisance''. Culverted, let into the sewers. The brook had marked the boundary between the parishes of Cardiff and Llandaf. In times of heavy rain and flood traces can still be seen pumping up through the street drains. Beneath the houses, deep piped, the Whitehouse, Nant-y-Ty-Gwyn, still flows. Dark. Unmissed.

Keep staring at the maps and you'll find other waters that no longer flow. The Golate, a stubby street running westwards from St Mary Street, was once a stream feeding the ancient, unstraightened Taf. There are Town records of waste dumped over it, drunks falling into it and petitions to have it unblocked. In Llandaf, the Mill Stream that ran from the Taf weir to course through the old graveyard and rejoin the main river at Pontcanna Fields flowed until 1952. It was drained when Llandaf Technical College was built on Western Avenue. The ditch of the stream's course remains for much of its length.

Chasing lost rivers is a peculiar obsession. In my experience an unshared one, mostly. I live in the east of Cardiff near the Roath Brook, otherwise known as the Lleici, the Licky, or the Nant Fawr[11]. Like city streets watercourses change their names along the length of their flow. This regular and powerful stream, with a rise and fall of between four and five feet that I've observed, starts in two places in the hills north of the city. The Llanishen branch (known locally as Llanishen Brook) rises under Graig Llanishen, near the old Hill Farm, and flows southwards to be joined, near Heath Halt railway station, by a tributary from the west. The eastern branch (the Nant Fawr) rises near Lisvane to flow through Llanishen Reservoir and on towards Roath Park, where it is joined by the outflow from Ffynnon Denis. The branches meet north of the wild gardens and, adopting their common name, the Lleici, course southwards through the long line of city parks. They flow east of St Margaret's Church to cross the Harlequin sports ground and, in new metal tunnels, slide below Sainburys and the Colchester Avenue Industrial Estate. The Lleici enters the Rhymney north of the David Lloyd Centre. This is how it has always flowed, hasn't it? Certainly not. My neighbour, a Church Warden at St Margaret's, mentioned to me one day that the basement of the Church House had become flooded. Where the Brook once flowed, before they moved it, she told me. Really?

The ordnance Survey 2.5 inch to the mile survey maps of the 1880s[12] show that when Roath Mill existed the leat followed the present brook's course. The real Lleici flowed to the south, through the gardens of the Sandringham Road houses, under Roath Church house, crossed by the stone slabs of the highway up Penylan Hill to Llwyn-y-Grant, to rejoin the mill stream in the centre of Waterloo Gardens. Traces are still visible, there's an island here, a cucumber spit of land rounded by two channels – one the mill stream the other the original river.

Checking the OS nineteenth-century survey further I found that the southern Lleici had its own collection of local tributaries, and many of them. This was moor land, after all. The most significant was the Wedal, a stream now largely lost to sight, which rose near Tonyrywen Farm on the Caerphilly Road – an area that once held Cardiff's first racecourse. This is now largely occupied by the St Isan, St Cadoc and St Ina roads, the Heath housing development and, of course, what remains of the Great Heath itself. The Heath, with boggy wood and pond at its centre and a wonderfully undeveloped air, stands large and underused, surrounded on three sides by housing development and to its south by the large University Hospital of Wales. Here, ever so briefly, the Wedal surfaces, emerging from a culvert to flow thin and straight across the common, bounded by wood strengthened banks and crossed by small metal bridges. It vanishes into the drains again on the north side of the hospital. Originally the Wedal went down what is now Eastern Avenue to join the main Lleici at Fairoak. The Juboraj is built on its course. The ancient bridge here was Pont Ieuan Quint. Lost, like the waterway it crossed. Another tributary rose near Ffynnon Bren between Penylan and Albany Roads, to run along the lane at the back of Marlborough Road and cross in front of St Margaret's church to join the Lleici there. The records at St Margaret's attest to an extension of the church yard being made down to the river bank. And the bridge, substantial enough, with arches and stone walls, can be seen in early photographs. Gone now. Like most lost rivers. First ditch. Sporadic ponding. Filled, covered. What's left piped.

The Lleici's course originally flowed south crossing Newport Road at the Burger King Drive-In to hit the Rhymney to the east of Pengam farm. Part of the dried watercourse is still there. Full of bramble. The brook a memory. The allotments beyond it are now that much drier. The real water silently moves beneath the feet of trolley pushers and the queues for Sainburys' row of cash machines.

Out walking, tracing the lost Lleici, I watch for ponding, unexpected drain covers, remade stone work, the land falling to where a ditch once might have been. With excitement and then careful note-taking I point my obsessive discoveries out to my partner. "The Lleici took a left here," I tell her. I can tell she's as interested as I am by the way she stares off into space.

Built On A Lost River
How Do you Know

drain covers lift after
rainfall

cellar fills

leaf

trees

moss
turf declining

map

memory

shapes of Africa rising
on the walls

bronchitis, ague, fever

your daintie nostrills
(in so hot a season, When
every clerke eates
artichokes and peason,
Laxative lettus, and
such windie meate)

surface ponding

overnight shoes
so white in the morning

the ghosts in the corridor

your bones
how they ache and swell
after storm

yes

the sound

notes

1. The black and white naturalist pamphlets I was brought up on never showed a hair out of place. When I first came upon it pubic hair was a shocking discovery. There was so much of it. For me this was like Oscar Wilde's reputed later-life discovery that women actually had legs beneath their all-enveloping waist to ankle skirts. He had thought them to possess only a single, inflexible trunk. For my part I'd imagined women featureless below the waist, like showroom dummies. This was how Harrison Marks depicted them, bounteous, waving their beach balls, smiling beneath their perms.
2. 'Advice to a Young Poet' – H. Webb, *Crown For Branwen*, Gomer 1974.
3. Intensive all-week Welsh language courses.
4. Government Publications.
5. The broad gauge had rails 7ft 0" apart. Very stable. It was abandoned in 1892 when the present-day 4ft 8" was accepted as the standard.
6. Half-cone boiler and Cardiff Bay International Superheater fitted December, 2000. Renamed John Osmond, January 2001.
7. Clwb Ifor Bach.
8. For a good sampler of how Champion Jack sounded in those days listen to *Champion Jack Dupree of New Orleans* on Storyville STCD 8015.
9. Cardiff Bridge, sometimes called Canton Bridge, crosses the Taf near Cardiff Castle. The present structure replaces an earlier wooden crossing made some 80 yards to the north, and dates from 1796. It was renovated mid nineteenth century with the addition of an iron balustrade and lamps.
10. Pontcanna, 'Canna's Bridge' in Welsh. Named after Saint Cana, the sixth-century daughter of Tewdwr Mawr (of St Tudor's, Mynyddislwyn) and the sister-in-law and disciple of St Illtud, the 'Master of Wales'. There's also a splendid rumour that she was a contemporary and even an associate of King Arthur. The Celtic Church in early Wales is full of such allusions. Cana may be buried under some Canton church or even in the washed-away graveyard of the first St Mary's. But I doubt it.
11. Edgar L. Chappell, early twentieth century Cardiff councillor and data obsessed local historian has traced dozens of names for Roath Brook starting with The Kenelech in 1200 and running through The Llyci, The Lliki, the Llecki, the Lleucu, the Lleici, and the Nant Mawr. At its northern extremities it's Nant yr Eglwys and Nant y Mynydd. On some OS maps it's called the Llechau (from Pont y Llechau – the bridge of flat stones, a name it has never born). Locals call it the Roath Brook. As a name the Lleici (after Saint Lleici or Lucy) is in retreat. Modern maps once again call it the Nant Fawr.
12. These highly detailed, well-drawn maps show every outbuilding and every tree. A local historian's dream.

WEST

CONIFER COURT

Landmarks are objects, conspicuous in the landscape, which the eye recognises and which, once seen, can often appear to follow you around. In the west the one you can't escape is the white golf-ball water tower on the ridge beyond St Fagans. On this side of the city the tower, like some local Fyllingdale radar watch, scans the skies for rogue intruders. Ely, Fairwater and Pentrebane lie dormant under its scrutinising eye.

Trying to reach the installation proves less than simple. High on the ridge that forms one side of the Ely valley (with the Ely estate itself on the other) the tower appears surrounded by scrub slope and crackling pine. There are no roads, no paths, no earth beaten tracks up through the trees. Below runs St Fagans Road connecting the housing estates of Fairwater with the folk life museum-dominated village of St Fagans, a vale of rural Cymrectitude stuck onto the edge of an industrial city. Here, just below the slope, stands Ty Bronna, an utterly unexpected example of charm and rural solidity, built by the art and crafts architect Charles Voysey, in 1903. The house, designed at the start of the Modern movement, reminds me of the sort of ideal mansion my parents would have sought, had they the money. Graceful, decorative arches along the south elevation, horizontal bands of windows, steeply hipped red-tile roof, white walls, battered buttresses, large chimneys. This is what happened to the Goths before the twentieth century turned their vision towards girder steel and ferro infill. Voysey built Bronna as a residence for landowner Hastings Watson. After the War it was converted into an ambulance

station. Now it's been restored again and sold on as a private house. There's no route from it to the tower. I drive slowly back in the direction of the city and turn, in order to try my luck, into the curving maze of Pentrebane.

This, of course, is where the tower is actually sited. At the top of Conifer Court, off Firs Avenue, west end of the estate. Getting here the route runs through shops, shuttered like

Beirut (this is a Sunday) spray painted and kicked to buggery, mostly food and alcohol – the *Pentrebane Fish Bar, K & K Londis,* the *Mini Market,* and, wonderfully hand painted with a five-inch wallpaper brush, *Sausage Thomas.* The Primary School windows are filled with kids' art work. The signs outside the community centre look like they've been shot at. There are hardly any parked cars.

But Pentrebane is not as wild as some parts of Cardiff. Today it's all sunlight and quiet. There is peach and cherry blossom on the trees. Old men with sticks walk overweight black dogs. A youth in track-suit bottoms and white t-shirt soaps a Fiesta. Someone's up a ladder fixing the gutters.

Up close the tower is white, dominant but not oppressive. It was originally built by the water board to add pressure to the mains in this part of the city. The higher up the hill the houses the more expensive it is to in pump in drinkable cold. Put a million gallons on top of a stick somewhere high above and your problem is solved. The structure has now been sold to Vodaphone. Its summit is festooned with rods, relays and repeaters. The sturdy fence protecting it has been vandalised. Inside, right below the white ball on its slender stem, are sheds filled with transmitters, boosters, fans and other telecom junk. On the side a neat sign tells me that radio transmissions are operated from this property. "For your own safety you are advised not to pass or stand within the hazard areas shown in red. Any requirement for persons to enter a hazard area should be by arrangement when the transmitter has been turned off." There's a plan of the spot where I'm standing in order to read the sign. I'm in one of the red bits. There's a telephone number to ring, in case of difficulty. Do I still feel ok? I call.

South Wales turns out to be in Vodaphone's Midlands division. A Birmingham-accented engineer, announcing himself as Central NMC, listens politely to my request for more information and then tells me that I'm calling on an internal line and he can't help. These phones are for engineers, he says. I apologise for not being one. Before I hang up I ask him what NMC stands for. Sorry, I can't tell you that, he replies. The Vodaphone Press Office are no more helpful. The woman there, the wrong side of flu by the sound of it, has no idea which tower I'm referring to and asks if it's made of lattice. No, it's like a giant white golf ball. Do you think it could be a radar installation? I ask provocatively. We always try to use existing structures, she sniffles, ignoring the jibe. Do the initials NMC mean anything to you? She ignores this too. She promises to find out more about the tower and call me back. She doesn't. Maybe it would have helped if I hadn't been calling her on Orange.

The drive back through Pentrebane skirts the farmland where Llandaf runs into Fairwater, site of the City's proposed post-2011, one-thousand dwelling development. Cardiff moves on out towards Bridgend and Llantrisant. The all-encompassing urban south Wales total-build of the future, like a novel by J.G. Ballard made real.

ELY

Ely is not a destination. You don't come here unless this is where you live. This is a mid-twentieth-century housing estate and it's huge. It's one of the largest in western Europe. Guarding the west of Cardiff, Ely stretches from the bridge over the river where Cowbridge Road meets Western Avenue to the Culverhouse Cross shopping malls and the media empire of HTV. I'm here to meet Steve Andrews, Bard of Ely, Quest Knight of the Loyal Arthurian Warband, Principal Bard of the Travelling Court of Camelot and member of the British Killifish Association. Cardiff might be my city but this is a slab of territory where I need a guide.

Until the end of the nineteenth century like much of the rest of greater Cardiff this was moorland. The village of Ely, a small cluster of cottages, an inn and a church, sat just to the west of the Ely River crossing. The land rising on slowly towards St Nicholas grazed cattle. South was unrelenting marsh until its clays became Leckwith and the quarries began. An earlier visit through the undergrowth along the precipitous sides of the almost culverted river had taken me past a "Don't Come In here" sign painted in raggy white on a tree trunk. The track led from the Bridge to the clay pits at Plymouth Woods, straight as a die. The Ely river had been realigned in the forties and sluiced between new higher banks to prevent the district (and Canton beyond it) from being constantly flooded. If you had a basement in this area then you kept fish. The path, rushing through bramble and beech, had taken me to the boggy bottom of Trelai Park the racecourse no one local ever referred to it by its cod-Welsh name. This was where the horses ran after the course had shifted here from the Heath in the early 1800s. Nothing on four legs now. Bar dogs. A bunch of middle-aged men in dark anoraks and mufflers were flying large radio-controlled planes from their spot in the centre of the

field. A five-foot winged Messerschmitt ME109 with Nazi markings buzzed me as I emerged from the trees. Here among the dandelions and the vivid rye had once stood a complete Roman villa: stores, latrine, outbuildings, bath house, verandah. In the times when Cardiff was no more than two huts and a fishing henge the Romans had marched through on their way west to Nidum[1]. They established a fort of the celtic shore by the Taf and this mansion in the middle of the wild Ely moors. There were more Romans than Welsh in Cardiff AD75. Those that are left now run the Italian grocers in Grand Avenue. Most of the Welsh have fled.

A few irregular bumps in the turf and a set of completely wrecked ferro-concrete park benches marking the outer limits are all now that remain of the villa. A pensioner with a terrier on a thirty-meter lead told me that he thought there were graves here. People with metal detectors come at night. They're not supposed to, he says, it's banned you know. Do they find anything? Yes. What? Don't know. Probably just bolts from the bust benches or old racing harnesses. Couldn't be anything of value after all this time, could it? Who but they will know. Under my foot is a loose turf. I kick it back. Half a rusted tin can. Lid illegible. There's a bi-plane above me now. Yellow wings. I watch it swoop, turn and then gracefully land.

Steve Andrews strides towards me at our appointed meeting place the Wilson Road shops. He's in his mid-forties with bald pate and Allen Ginsberg wizard hair. He's lived here twenty years and makes a living as a writer and musician. His new single, *Nicky Wire You're a Liar*, a disco-mix rhythmic complaint about the prices the Manics chose to charge for drinks at their see-the-Millennium-in bash at the

Stadium has just been banned by Spillers, Cardiff's greatest independent record shop. How will you sell it now, I ask. Internet. Steve is already number two in the Cardiff area mp.3.com folk charts. The only way on is up.

The immense estate of council housing that is now Ely (and its immediate southerly neighbour – Caerau) largely went up between the wars. New houses were first built on the Red House Farm in 1923 and by 1939 the estate as it is now was mostly in place. Clustered at the city end were its industries – the paper mills, the breweries, Chivers Pickle factory, the rail links, the hospital. Along the edge of the rising Leckwith escarpment were the brickworks and the barrage balloon hangers. Nothing left now. Even the Distribution Centre, the light industrial estate hastily introduced as a sop to local mass unemployment is largely empty. The district bears all the marks of indifference. Untended grass verges, snapped saplings, graffiti, burned-out cars, smashed bus-shelters, blowing paper, scarred brickwork, boarded houses, shuttered shops. Without work, who cares.

When it was built Ely was expensive. Class design, quality build, electric lighting when the rest of the city ran on gas, wide streets, grass, trees and two parallel, dramatic boulevards in the north Grand Avenue and below that Heol Trelai. There was a clamour to get in now there's a clamour to leave.

Steve takes me to his place, gloriously celebrated in Chris Stone's *Last of the Hippies*. We turn past the bread shop where the riots began on a steaming hot night ten years back. Nobody died but the district was curfewed for seven nights, buildings were burned down and armed police were bussed in from as far away as the Met. Bricks. Bottles. Firebombs. Looting. Arrests. White vs Asian. Insider vs. outsider. Bad bad feelings that persist. There's a lane running along the back of the buildings that is as wide as the one in which the fire of London started. Who uses these? Everyone.

In Parker Place Steve's front room is a seventies time capsule. The walls are covered with cards, snaps and clippings. Marijuana leaf icons. Biker poetry. Standing stones. Three shots of Bridget St John at the seaside. Crop circles. Glastonbury banners. Band posters. Beards. Beads. The Captain. Rainbows. King Arthur's Sword. When he stays that's Arthur's bed, says Steve, pointing at the brown and rather battered couch. Arthur who, I ask? Arthur Pendragon. When we go to the pub he goes in full regalia his green cape, his crown, his bag, his holy lance and, of course, Excalibur. He likes a drink. He's very popular with kids. That's the spot where Lionel Fanthorpe was knighted into the Loyal Warband. Steve points at a table covered with books and manuscripts. Right there. Quite a moment. Does Arthur visit often? Now and then.

We set off for the Dusty Forge Community Centre and Steve tells me that he's following up his Herbs of the Northern Shaman – *A Guide to Mind-Altering Plants of the Northern Hemisphere* (Loompanics) with a guide to the herbs of Venus and Mars. Thorsons are interested. I'm doing the Martian ones, he says. Those are plants with spikes or red berries like stinging nettles and Butcher's Broom. Strong plants. There's one, a celandine, that's Martian. He points into an overgrown grass verge. Ayla, she's a witch, is handling the Venusian side. You can split the entire plant kingdom this way. It'll be a useful work. It will.

At the Dusty Forge, which used to be a pub until the council refused to renew its licence on account of the fighting, we meet with Peter, a mid-forties Ely resident with no visible tattoos and an overpowering desire to show us around. You want to know the real Ely, he says, I'll show you. We climb into his low-slung Cavalier and roar off up Wheatley Road. Peter wants to show us the bloody stupid hundred-thousand-a-go build of posh houses they've put at the top of Mostyn Road. This tight development of mock-Georgian residences is another Persimmon investment called Westfield Park. The views from it, across the green-belt fields to Llanmaes Farm and St Fagans beyond are idyllic. A major factor in Persimmon's game plan, no doubt. What they hadn't counted on, of course, was the use of their new development by Ely locals as a short cut between the Rec and Penmark Road. Car slash and bricks of envy and disgust through windows. We cruise brand new Celandine Road – every other property has a For Sale board standing like a sentinel outside.

Peter's driving could have come directly from Hollywood. One arm enveloping the steering wheel, the other out of the open window, fag in hand. The car sinks low on its suspension as we round corners

and bounce up lanes. Every now and then we pass small groups of
men idling slowly with cans in hand, or sprawled across walls with
glazed looks on their faces. How's it going bro, what's happenin.
Catch you later. Those were the Wilson Boys, Peter says. We pass a
group who look like they've been partying for days. Sway, stumble,
dance, fall down. We head for Birdie's Lane which connects Ely with
Fairwater. That's Rocky's Gym. Peter points at a pre-fab styled hall
set in trees. Ray Thorogood trains there. Boxing has always been big
in the west of Cardiff. The car goes up a track that looks barely wide
enough to take a push chair. With skill Peter spins us round narrowly
missing an earth embankment. This is the top of Ely, he says, pointing out across the valley towards the white golf-ball water tower in
Pentrebane. Now for the bottom.

The bottom turns out to be Caerau. We reach it via the site of the
Regent Cinema, (now the Regency Nursing Home), and the Grovers
Terrace houses of 1881 the oldest in Ely, Peter is sure. Finally, we
swing around the back of the hospital (now flats) to barrel along
broad Heol Trelai to reach the Cwrt yr Ala Road asbestos disaster.
This is a spike-roofed run of boarded-up link houses about the size
of stair cupboards now awaiting space-suited men to arrive and pull
them down. What's the biggest problem here, I ask? Travel. There are
no buses after 7.30 pm because the kids stone them. Some old bloke
got his head full of glass and the driver was taken to hospital. Do you
think it's as rough here as it used to be? No. It's worse. No respect for
women. Wasn't like that when I was a kid. We roll up Hill Fort Drive
to be deposited at the foot of the Caerau Iron Age Stronghold.
According to CADW this is one of the largest multivallate hillforts in
south-east Wales – an impressive stretch of huge embankment,
massive earth defence and deep external ditch. It's stuffed now
between the southern edge of endemic vandalism and the Ely link
dual carriage way. We emerge from the houses to be faced with its
bulk. Its clodded sides are covered with wreckage, prams, bust
fridges, burned mattress, bramble that's been shat in, stunted trees
that have been ripped and mangled, sprawls of builders waste, broken
red-brick, ash, dust, crap. Climbing it is an effort. This iron age
defence was made to last.

On top, inside the circled ditches, are the remains of a twelfth
century Norman ringwork. As a variation on the usual castle mound
with a wooden keep on top the walls of the existing iron age fort here
were re-used. Why build when you don't have to? Ely stretches out
beyond us. Huge and threatening. But there's not much you can do

to earthworks, so long as you don't own a bulldozer. Grass will grow back if you dig. The scars of estate shittery will mend. But the damage done to the thirteen century St Mary's Church is now utterly unfixable. This ancient parish church, with its saddleback roofed tower set in the Fort's centre, had stood, cherished and used, for eight-hundred years. Over the centuries it had been regularly restored, making good what time and the weather did. In 1959 the Reverend V.H. Jones began what was to be its final refurbishment. He'd raised enough to fix the windows, fill the wall cracks and put the roof back on. An ancient crypt full of bones was found and sealed over. Medieval wall paintings in the nave were restored. In 1961 the Church was re-consecrated by the Bishop of Llandaf. But by the 70s ruin had returned. Wrecking raids on the graveyard and attacks on the church fabric welled up from the buzzing Caerau boredom below and continued sporadically for the next thirty years. Walls fell, were pushed, dug under, burned. Gravestones were uprooted. Slabs were cracked. In the 90s caravans and tents were pitched. The stone work that still stood was painted in dazzle colour. Raves rocked through the night. When I visited in the 80s the ruin still looked church-like. There were four walls, fragments of roof on the tower. Today it's a heap of rubble with just one westerly wall fenced back and just about erect. Smashed memorials mix with churned earth, beer can and nettle. Desecration has been championed to Hiroshima proportion. If a ley ever radiated through here it has now been truncated. Even the air feels broken. These sites leach something of their power into whatever it is that is built over them, says Steve. I wish they did. Anywhere else an historic centre as rare as this one would be preserved, restored, venerated. We both look out north over the streets full of dogs and men sitting on low walls smoking. Pub next. What else?

GRANGETOWN

There's an air of last century Poland about Grangetown – invaded by outsiders, districts fought over, sections sliced off, parts renamed and given to others. Today buses bound here have the words *Cardiff Bay* across their destination boards. Paranoia has set in. Grangetown was built largely in the late 1800s, across the silt of the Leckwith and West Moors. It was part of a shambling plan to sell housing to coal cutters at the docks, railway workers, and middle managers at the local

bakehouses, builders yards and brickworks. The original proposal, to exploit the Bute and Windsor bridges over the Taf and Ely and the new Penarth Road by developing an industrial district based around the Penarth Iron and Steel Works, collapsed in 1881 when that venture closed. Grangetown became a suburb you could walk from the town of Cardiff and Bute's ever expanding docks. It's bounded by two rivers – the Ely to the West and the Taf to the East. To the north is the Cardiff to Swansea rail line and the start of Canton. To the south lies the sea.

Upper Grangetown – originally called Saltmead, an area inundated by sea at high tide – centred on the Tannery at Gillards Field (now Sevenoaks Park). Lower Grangetown was on the drained flats near the gas works. Thirty years of housebuilding bridged the mile or so of open country which separated the two villages. By 1900 Grangetown was a Cardiff suburb with a population of 17,000; donkeys in the back kitchens, pigs in the passages, chickens in the yards and some of the best sewers anywhere in the expanding town.

Before the industrial age all that was here was a farm. There are records of a grange[2] in this area going back a thousand years, a fact that the locals are much more proud of than the city itself which has systematically pulled down all its ancient farmsteads. This is the last one. Grange Farm kept cattle for milk until as late as 1914. Its fields were sold for housing, to build the library, the laundry, to put in Clive Street, a wide Grange boulevard running south to the bay. I'm in Grangetown with Dave Coombs, probation officer, born here. Once again guides are good although Dave has not been back much for forty years. We're standing outside the farm house, sunk three feet below street level, angled at thirty degrees to the road, whitewashed, ancient, unmarked. CADW won't take it on, Eileen Breslin tells us, not decreed as important enough. She's chair of the Grangetown History Society and keeps an eye on the local monument from her house in Stockland Street. We get a tour of the Society's records, on show at the library next door, where Dave spots his father in a shot of the Grange Baptists RFC 1921-22 side. Grainy po faces. Poor focus. That's his shirt. Dave can tell. As a sect the Baptists were a sociable group, unlike the Gospel thumping Plymouth Brethren who imagined sport to be pretty near dancing on the route to perdition and banned its adherents from ever taking part.

Eileen introduces us to Nigel Sutton, the present owner of the farm, who moved here from Bridgend not because of any sense of history but because the place had a garden. Cardiff housing stock is not well blessed with space for tree studded lawns and rolling herbaceous border. Nigel has filled the yard with potted hosta and fashionable bamboo. The farm well goes down more than thirty feet, he's had a look. Full of masonry and potshards, wooden cover on top. The house with its exposed wooden beams, medieval archways and fragments of gothic tracery feels like it should be full of ghosts. Instead Nigel's union steel guitar lies against the sofa and blues CDs stack up against the wall. He reckons that what we are standing in is a sixteenth century barn conversion rather than a twelfth century relic. Grade II listed, better than nothing. There's no plaque, Nigel's fixing his own to the garden wall.

Along Clive Street we pass Tôpher Mills' house where for much of the eighties and nineties he published his Red Sharks poetry books using an Atari Games Machine and strong carpet glue. Geoff Hattersley and Ian Macmillan made their Cardiff debuts as Tôpher pamphlets, as did local writers Ifor Thomas, John Harrison, Jackie Aplin, John Hindle, Pat Egan and others. Tôpher's desperate ambition to be larger than life bore fruit in the late nineties when outsize outfitters High & Mighty employed him to launch their new

store. Tôpher's industrial presence and enthralling delivery were perfect. The difficult moment came when H&M promotional vouchers were tied to balloons filled with helium. Instead of rising to the skies the now heavier than air flyers rolled out across the road to be punctured by passing cars. Tôpher was paid in jackets and boots. His appearances on stage these days, as Cardiff

performance poet par excellence, are enhanced by red shoes and drape jackets of quality and dimension not usually seen in the world of verse. There's no one in when we ring the bell. This is morning and it's a hard life. Tôpher sleeps.

We pass the Ebenezer Gospel Hall, built 1899, and now so shuttered, barred and intruder alarmed that you'd imagine there were vast ecclesiastical riches within rather than wooden benches and stacks of well-thumbed good books. A sign outside advertises meetings of the Sunbeams Club, the Ladies Afternoons and the 'J' Zone. Along the road stands the Salvation Army Church. Women in saris push prams along the pavements. There's a bloke in knitted hat and dreadlocks fixing an oily bike. Opposite someone has a notice on their door which reads NO JEHOVAS WITNESS. It is done in a Christmas card typeface with snow settled on the upper half of the letters. The next dozen or so doors have signs in Arabic script above them which tell us that Allah Is Great.

Down into the Ferry Road peninsula, deep Lower Grange, below the Marl playing fields and the new Bay drainage pumping station, the streets narrow to become humped and traffic calmed. There's a high rise here, Channel View Flats, and a whole raft of debris-filled gardens, bin bags and trashed bus shelters. We're near the bay but reaching it is hard. Between here and Asda, where the Ferry Road car dismantlers once operated, a slice of the district has gone, annexed by developers. This is now the walled, almost-gated, orange brick, waterside housing development of Windsor Quay. No trash. No overgrown hedges. No graffiti. No dumped hard core. These are The Cairns – Kestrel Drive, Campbell Drive, Constant Close. Not a Welsh place name among them. When it comes to the Bay Cymraeg has proved itself not to be a selling point. You can't get here by road from Lower Grangetown. The way in is to leave and re-enter from the south.

Will Hutton, the journalist, economist and broadcaster, has a theory that what he calls the *hot networks*, the rising desirable, economically vibrant inner city developments, live cheek by jowl with *cold networks* the depressed and vandalised, uncared for under-invested districts. The two barely touch. Interaction is zero. In south Grangetown it's pretty frosty.

Half a block into Windsor Quay and suddenly, man, it's hot.

Beyond lies the Red House, Cardiff's most southerly pub, only open in the evening now the car wreckers and parts recyclers have been shifted. There's a security hut, barrier and guard. He protects the peninsula point yacht club and the land the city intend to develop, once they raise the money, as a sports village: snowdome, pool, stadium, basketball, ice rink, hockey, drive-thrus, shopping malls and other essentials. How long will that take, I ask. Ten years if we're lucky. We're passed by a stream of Mercs and BMWs, driven by well-tanned middle-agers wearing moustaches and polo shirts. The club is exclusive. Can we stroll down and take a look? More than my job's worth. He does some classic headshaking. Dave and I, we look like vandals. Obviously. There's a swan and cygnets nested among the bay's edge reed growth. Cleaner water here than at Roath Park. Behind the nest is a spiral stone jetty left by the road builders. It's been sold for several million to Bellway Homes who will water barrier, drain and build enough housing to get their investment back ten fold. Marina town houses. Maritime balconies. Chandlers Drive. Pilot Place. Will they still call it Grangetown? What do you think.

HADFIELD ROAD

South-west of the city in the once great flood plain between the estuaries of the Taf and the Ely lies Hadfield Road. This smooth and underused stretch of metalled highway connects the old Penarth road with the newer A4232 which cuts up out of Cardiff to join the M4 to the north. Standing here now, looking over the tarmac-crossed flats, with their mix of fast-build low-rise warehouse and glass-fronted block-walled show units you might be mistaken for imagining that water never got this far. But it did. As recently as last century these were the West Moors – a land of river gravel overlaid with waterlogged clay and rough grass; rifted with reens, sluices and ponds. Like the rest of the present city, it seems you farmed here if you had good boots or a boat.

Hadfield Road is Cardiff's answer to mid-west America. No one walks it. No skateboards. No dogs on leads. The pavements are clear from start to finish. In the several hours I prowled its length I didn't see anyone who didn't arrive precisely at their destination by car. Draw up, open the door, stroll ten yards. That's what this is. Drive-in auto land. Hadfield is car showrooms run together on the me-too principle from Plexiglas beginning to crystal laminated end. Inside, the ubiquitous salesmen are all mid-Cardiffian clones clever enough to catch the big spenders, patient enough to work the economy end. These guys could sell anything anywhere in the Capital. They're swift, slick and they smile. They sell to couples with babies, middle-aged fatties in trainers and track suit bottoms, tieless youths in big shirts. At VW, where style and image have become everything, they are in suits and you are sir. At Honda they wear polo shirts and call you mate. They put you at ease, offer you coffee, press brochures in your hands. Prices have fallen, things are tough, commission is hard to find. There's a guy outside Mazda in a Chrysler Voyager People Carrier in which he has installed sixteen speakers and is blasting out garage at more than 100 decibels. He has the windows down. No one tells him to stop.

We are in sight here of a whole bunch of past Cardiff landmarks. Grange Farm. Canton Moor. Leckwith Bridge. Bessemer Road and its Sunday market. Ninian Park, where the fans of the club that once actually roared up through the First Division are now among the most violent in Britain. Check their fanzines to experience the sprawling, half-literate violence that blows over soccer like a dark cloud. But they are not in Hadfield Road buying racers, GTIs, hot hatches, not today.

In the vast Fiat customer car park, full of white vans and coupés, it begins to rain. A herring gull in its second winter plumage lands near a parked Brava and, looking lost for a moment, tilts its head, stares under the tyres. This bird breeds on cliffs and moorland. It would have been here well before the Italian car maker. Before there was an Italy. Before Rome, come to that. It takes off through the Cardiff drizzle, still doing it after thousands of years. It heads south towards Daihatsu. Why walk. There's no point.

KING'S CASTLE

The competition is tight. Which is the largest American state? In cricket a score of one-one-one is known as what? Name a 1970s Clint Eastwood film in which he sings. Our team, we are called *I Bought This Jacket In A Jumble Sale*, have got the answers down for

everything except for the constituents of feta cheese. Don, the magis-
trate, is sucking the end of his pen. Across the room the residents
wave their arms and shout. There's a lot of fervour here. This is the
Mandeville House Probation and Bail Hostel quarterly quiz.
Mandeville is in Lewis Street where Riverside merges with Canton,
the houses are neat and tight, and the pavements are swept clean
every day. The Bail Hostel is a midpoint between incarceration and
freedom. The inmates, they are actually called *residents*, can spend
their days under the sky but are required to spend their nights under
lock and key. They are a mix of burglars, murderers, robbers and
rapists. There's hardly a white-collar criminal among them. Some
have that thin white look you only get from twenty years out of the
sun. Most sport home-made tattoos and t-shirts with the sleeves cut
off at the shoulder. Their team are taking the quiz far more seriously
than anyone else. We put down sheep's milk. They opt for ewe's. It's
a tough call. We are neck and neck. The question master, a chief
probation officer on his night off and sporting the loudest tie I've
seen since 1956, lets them have it. They woop and dance. The prize
is a 500g bar of Cadbury's Milk. Alcohol is banned. On my way in I
was met by a rubber-gloved assistant manager with a fist of syringes.
Upstairs toilets, he said to me, as if I was in the know. The chocolate
is held high, as if it were a flag. We clap and drink our tea. Why not.

Mandeville's fund raisers – the quiz, one of their efforts, you pay
a fiver to enter – do good works for charity and among the local
population. This to help ameliorate the effect of two dozen ne'er-do-
wells tramping their streets and dropping litter on their flowers. A
recent scheme was Bikes for Bosnia with cycles rebuilt by the
residents using donated parts and frames rescued from the council
tip. To get here I've put my Ford in the snooker hall car park which
separates Mandeville from Cowbridge Road. It won't get locked in.
Rileys never shuts. Here, in the dark hours the cigarette smoke drifts
across the down-lit tables. Solemn mouthed young men chalk their
cues, imagining themselves, one more time, to be Paul Newman,
decimating the opposition. Inscrutable, silent. Like poker this game
runs best when the rest of the world has closed. At Mandeville the
residents sleep the sleep of the just. They can do little else.

In the rest-room Mike, the duty manager, is stirring his mug of tea
with a pen. He is idly watching the b&w monitor which shows
Mandeville's double-doored entrance and small forecourt. His
Cortina sits there. Not much but paid for, his old pullover on the

back seat. It's a dry night. Suddenly, from around the corner roars a
JCB, demolishing one Manderville gate pillar and gouging the other
as it comes. It is manned by a raged resident out to let the system
know who's boss. The trenching bucket swings menacingly, catches
Mike's car by the front axle and hurls it into the air. It lands with a
Hollywood smash of crumpling metal and shattering glass. At first
Mike fails to recognise what has happened. Then slowly, appalled, he
does. The JCB sways, turns and powers up for an assault on the main
doors. The gears mesh. The look on the face of the driver is glazed
malice. But the duty manager has acted. Alerted police and hostel
officers rush in to overpower the malcontent. Reason is pointless.
There's a struggle, brief, some shouting, and then the engine dies. A
last brick falls with a measured crack. Mike surveys the scene with
measured disbelief. Everything over as soon as it began. Bugger. His
tea mug cools, silently filling with ink from his teaspoon pen.

The walk to the pub through the calm evening takes us past the
boarded up St David's Hospital with its slowly fragmenting
signboard. Sheenagh Pugh, the poet whose territory this very much
is, celebrated the facility's rise and fall in the title of one of her books,
Id's Hospit. It's a burned shell, a Cardiff institution lost now in the
collective memory as much as Ely Racecourse or the Timber float.
The Victorians built St David's in 1839 as the Cardiff Union
Workhouse. It could hold 1,800 inmates. It offered them food,
charity, bed but all at a standard below the most menial obtainable
outside. You went in here only if you had to. But many still did.

We are headed for the King's Castle, a pub standing at the very
heart of old Canton. The original village was little more than a cross,
a manor house, a farm and a cluster of cottages just to the north of
Canton pool and common. This is the area currently occupied by the
houses running south from Brunswick Street to Landsdowne Road
and the main rail line west to Swansea. The original King's Castle, a
tavern and great house, stood a bit to the west of the present edifice.
It was erected on a natural mound. During the Civil War when the
Royalists had holed up in Cardiff Castle, Cromwell brought his
troops here. Cannons were set. The Roundheads pulled ale from the
King's Castle barrels. Would they storm the town's West Gate from
this comfortable base? In the event their battle took place in the war
horse fields around St Fagans. In 1648 Cromwell's cavalry under
Colonel Horton routed 8,000 Royalists. Many died. The Ely ran with
their blood. In the centuries since bones have been disinterred at
roadsides, fragments of pikestaff found by ploughs and shattered

helmets removed from the roots of trees. Ironically, Wales is now a left-leaning monopoly with power in the hands of either the socialists or the nationalists with hardly a unionist in sight. But in the seventeenth century it was a Royalist stronghold. Hard to imagine today. Cromwell and his parliamentary revolutionists had an uphill battle.

The present King's Castle appears not to have changed since the early sixties. It has a coffee brown ceiling, a quarter-moon arc of a wooden bar and tables set in booths. We take the corner. There are beer mats, rare enough. An Irish couple loudly go at each other two tables down. No one reacts. I order lager, vodka tonic, fizzy water. The lager's off, there's no tonic but I could have pineapple. And still water only, our apologies, from the tap. I go back later and try for crisps. Sorry, this is Wednesday. My fault, so it is. I order bitter. He shakes his head slowly and gives a resigned smile. Barrel's gone. Would you manage with a bottle of India Pale? The Irish couple are shouting now. The woman, shaggy headed and in a coat which envelops her form entirely is half-standing and thumping the table. No one looks. What drives their passion? Love? It can't be the drink.

Just beyond the King's Castle is Chapter, the city arts centre based at the converted Canton High School in Market Road. Established in 1969 by the trio of Mik Flood, Chris Kinsey and Bryan Jones, Chapter has ploughed an alternative arts furrow now for more than thirty years. It has great strengths in the visual arts, in theatre and especially in cinema. Without it, Cardiff artistic life would have been persistently poorer. Geoff Moore's *Moving Being*, almost entirely a Chapter creation, was the single Welsh live-art beacon during the unenlightened seventies. Today Chapter policy still sparks. In a building reorganised and restructured many times over the air of cutting-edge activity remains palpable. In the bar they have something like forty-eight different single malts. They sell Czech beer and that dreadful Belgian stuff with chocolate in it. Some of Europe's greatest theatre companies have tried to sample them all.

What Chapter can't manage well is poetry. As an institution there is something about the place which puts distance between management and activity. Poets are forever finding themselves confounded by technicians who won't let them move furniture, bring drinks into the auditorium, adjust the lights or turn down the music. By default some events take place here because there is nowhere else quite suitable. Cardiff is a city of brushed aluminium bars, house music, and kids so full of alcopop they cannot speak. Venues suitable for verse are hard to find. Chris Torrance, the *Magic Door* renegade from the Beacons waterfall country, ran the *South Wales Poetry Society* here with Barry Edgar Pilcher and Phil Maillard during the distant seventies. Son of the famous *No Walls* readings, *Horse*, with Fred Daly and Peter Huw Morgan, the slide-guitar slinging bard of Canton, was here briefly before that. During the eighties *Cabaret 246* put just about everyone in the city with a voice, a poem and the ability to put the two together onto the black, smoke-ridden stage in the downstairs bar. The atmosphere was so thick then that when you got home you had to hang your coat on the line in the rain just to remove the stink. Put out by perceived male dominance the women successfully formed *Deadlier Than The Male* and, later, inevitably, its splinter group, *Pandora's Box*. Chapter stopped them moving the furniture too. In the nineties Cab turned to Slam. The audience increased exponentially as it became clear that anyone and everyone could have their piece of fifteen-second fame on stage here, in front of half-cut, roaring crowds. In the late nineties the tradition has been continued with super-slick productions from Lloyd Robson, Chris Brooke and Steve Prescott's *Sampler* featuring some of the best of south Wales's literary performers. When I went last year they were playing old jazz between poets, handing out verse booklets as part of the ticket price and had beer mats on the tables. There was strong evidence that furniture had been moved about. I had a Speyburn. No one stopped me taking it in. Things have changed.[3]

I saw Yevtushenko here decades back. At that time Russia was still vitally soviet and a dark and very suppressed place. Yevgeny was their one international cultural allowance. Half a rebel. An approved protester who travelled with three KGB minders, a girlfriend, and a translator. His English was perfect but the readings were in Russian with the English version always read by someone else. Yevgeny, noble looking, tall and thin, would stand listening to his words come back in surreally altered form (he fervently supported metrical vigour but the translations were into loose, free verse) and then nod before launching off into Russian again. At the end the crowd, most of whom had no idea where Stantsiya Zima was nor the significance of Babi Yar[4], were allowed questions. What have you buggers done with Solzhenitsyn, shouted a man wearing the broken rifle badge of War Resistors International, off the point, or maybe right on it. There was no answer. The minders spoke into Yevgeny's ear. He smiled and took a different question. Everyday, he said. I write everyday. Writing is work. Not freedom. It's a thing that has to be done.

Outside the streets are dry. A straightened river rushes along the side of Trelai Park. The waters flow between concrete edgings. The Canton Moors no longer flood. The Castle is fifteen minutes walk away. We head there.

ST FAGANS

Not a Welsh name but perhaps the Welshest of places in the whole city. Saint Fagan was an Italian missionary sent by the Pope in 140 to convert the local tribes. Christianity was hot and violent then. The Pope's reach was stretched. The chapel dedicated to Fagan, or the remains of it, is still there in the castle grounds. And absolutely unique. There is only one St Fagans anywhere in the world. This is it.

The place, of course, is not primarily known for its ancient village, for the great battle against the Roundheads, nor really for the castle itself – a fine Elizabethan manor house with castellations high on its walls. St Fagans is a miniature of rural Wales set on the western edge of Cardiff. Landscaped onto a bluff guarding the River Ely and high above the beech, oak and ash which cloak the rail main line, St Fagans is a miracle of tranquillity in close proximity to flurry. This is the great outdoor National Museum of Welsh Life – 105 acres of pathway, copse, green lane, hedge, stonewall and step connecting more than forty original Welsh buildings dismantled, transported and rebuilt here, brick by authentic brick.

The problem for Cardiffians has always been remembering that they have this treasure in their midst. When it was established in 1946 St Fagans was little more than a period house with a couple of galleries added showing old farm implements, a few hay carts and a bunch of decayed Welsh pots. Folk life. The life of folk. You brought your visitors here. You rarely came yourself. This is how life is outside the city, you'd say. Now you've seen it we don't have to go. When the Museum began adding outbuildings trucking the numbered stones in, re-erecting them in precisely the right order, lighting wood fires in their grates, and installing Welsh speaking keepers to guard them the life depicted turned out to be one for which urban Wales did not have that much sympathy. Hendre'r-Ywydd Uchaf, Llainfadyn Cottage, the Maentwrog hayshed and the rest came from a Wales most Cardiff locals had never seen and cared about even less. The Museum issued an 00 scale card model of their Hendre medieval timber-framed farmhouse. Cheap – but Cardiff schoolboys who usually went for this kind of thing did not include it in their Hornby Double-O layouts. Things got worse when the Museum began to raise its entrance charges. St Fagans turned into an expensive destination. Penarth cost less. The pier cost pennies. Roath Park Lake was even cheaper. The prom there was free.

But over the ensuing decades dedicated and, to judge by present day results, absolutely enlightened staff, continued their policy of preserving vanishing Welsh culture by shifting it in on the back of lorries. The rusticity of the Museum's principle interests moved from the backwoods village to the rural township – a bakehouse arrived, so did a tailor's shop, a post office, Bridgend's 1880 Gwalia Stores, a summer house from Bute Park, and then, spectacularly in 1987, Rhyd-y-Car, a complete terrace of iron worker's houses from Merthyr Tydfil. This Richard Crawshay built line of half a dozen cottages was installed to illustrate different periods of their history the earliest, flag floor, God He Watchest Thee plates on the mantle shelf, from 1805 the most recent, carpet, MFI kitchen, colour TV and Betamax video, from 1985. The Museum experienced a culture shift. Visitors who remembered the original cottages, some who'd even lived there, began to turn up. The Museum of Folk Life had moved nearer to the people.

More recently St Fagan's has added an aluminium prefab bungalow from Cardiff's Gabalfa estate, Newbridge's War Memorial, and the entire Oakdale Workmen's Institute building complete with committee rooms, toilets, concert hall and library. Behind glass cases the books line – Herbert Matthews' *Eyewitness in Abyssinia*, W. J. Gruffydd's *Hen Atgofion*, Lord Riddell's *Some Things That Matter*, The Letters of Queen Victoria and, lest they forget, Prof W.S. Boulton's six volume *Practical Coal Mining*. I listen in as two former pit workers, squat, trainers, jackets from 1960s Burton suits, excitedly point out to each other just where they used to sit. In the corner the keeper dozes in his folding chair. These visitors knew more about Oakdale's history than he.

My visit co-incides with the Museum's Gwyl Fihangel, its Harvest Festival, entirely free now that the Assembly has insisted the institution drop entrance charges. Since this progressive piece of legislation visitor numbers have doubled. At the recreated Celtic village (wattle walls, palisade and ditch) I slide past the Silures, a hippie-looking bunch of iron age re-creators done up in sackcloth, knitted things, beads and bent on cooking fish and veg broth in a giant open air pot.

Hidden in a corner I spot a sandwich box under a pile of straw. Two chubby warriors chat in west country English. There are plenty of kids but no dogs. The official keeper, shaved head, small earring, tells me the Celts are a great success but they only come here on special weekends.

Round the corner from the St Fagans House of the Future, the result of a competition to suggest how we might all be living in a permanent recycling loop fifty years from now, is the Glamorgan Iron Horse Vintage Society's open-air exhibition of old farm machinery. Steam driven hay bundlers, butter churners, power saws and other rattling mechanicals whir and putter. They are contentedly tended by their smiling, overweight owners. Pipes are smoked. A hay thresher's wife, sitting in a deck chair, eats a sandwich. A goose pecks the grass. Inside the marquee erected to house the Welsh Food producers road show, the Pigs Folly Welsh Sausage Experience appears to be outselling Pemberton's Chocolate Lovespoons. Celtic Country Wines' Bootlegger's Moonshine Vodka faces down Celia's Oriental Kitchen. Celia herself is in action heating up and flogging stuff with noodles. Ralph is offering samples of his 7.2% dry cider. His tape player is belting out American rock. I buy a Welsh lamb-burger encased in traditional Welsh bap. Outside two musicians dressed as Laurel and Hardy play Elvis. Folk life has shifted quite a lot.

At the Castle itself, past Neville Thomas demonstrating coracle work across the fish ponds, his rucksack containing a pork pie and a piece of cheese hanging on a waterside post, I buy teisen lap and PG Tips in the traditional tea rooms. The women on the next table are talking about their husband's operations. A youth comes in demanding coke and crisps but there are none. No face painting nor bouncy castle either. The new view of folk life continues to have style.

At Capel Pen-Rhiw, y Parchedig Aled Gwyn leads a service. This is Sunday and it *is* the harvest festival. Raggy voices rise within. A latecomer tries the door but is defeated, the tiny chapel is full. And this is all still Cardiff. Really. It is.

notes

1. Nidum now Neath. The Roman remains there are covered by roads, playing fields and a housing estate.
2. A grange is properly the *granum*, the granary or farm of a monastery.
3. Since writing this Sampler itself has closed. The publishers of this book, Seren, have started their own series. Nothing stays still for long.
4. Babi Yar is the name of a ravine near Kiev where many thousands of Jews were massacred and buried during the Second World War.

NORTH

CASTELL COCH

At the river crossing where the Taf squeezes itself between the final pair of south Wales hills before snaking out like an unheld hose pipe across the Cardiff alluvial flats, stands a fairy-tale castle. In the Tongwynlais beech woods, among the wild garlic, high above the golf course and the drinkers at the Lewis Arms, stands Castell Coch – The Red Castle – called so because of the colour of its walls. Its perfectly slated, conical roofs look like something directly from Hollywood. It can't be real. It's not. This is another Bute-powered, Burges recreation; a fantasy made real one hundred and fifty years ago beyond the industrial squalor of Cardiff. While hard-won coal headed for the sea down the valleys the Marquis used his enormous wealth to exercise his particularly Victorian obsession – making the medieval real. With the aid of architect William Burges he had already built for himself one illusory palace, in the town centre, Cardiff Castle. Now he wanted a country retreat. Castell Coch, lost in the woodland, hard to climb to, was perfect.

Many imagine this whole edifice to be no more real than the dinosaur park at Dan yr Ogof but Burges's creation is built on genuinely medieval foundations. The towers might be a little higher than they should be and the dungeon a nineteenth century extravagance but what lies underneath them is indisputably ancient. Originally this was a Gilbert de Clare piece of thirteenth century insurance, built around 1266 when the Normans were big in Glamorgan and the Welsh, under Llywelyn, were determined to have a go at knocking them down. Llywelyn had already given the enemy a bloody nose with his successful wall-smashing attack on Caerphilly. Check it out, the glorious evidence is still visible today. As extra defence the Normans put Castell Coch up fast. However, what is left of that original creation today is not very much. As at Cardiff Castle itself such ancient remains as there are have all been incorporated into the contemporary build. Bits of medieval masonry can been seen in Castell Coch's well tower and below its great drawbridge. The rest is mostly nineteenth-century addition. But Castle spotters love this place. It's compact. It's complete. The rain doesn't get in. You can see all its history without walking too far. It's not constricted by other buildings and there are no intrusive souvenir sellers. As an attraction it's virtually perfect.

There are some who imagine this place to be one of the seats of that legendary uniter of Avalon, King Arthur of the Brits. I tell this to

Mami Ando, a young Japanese touring the world with a footloose determination better than that of W. H. Davies and currently coping with Wales. She wants to kiss the Blarney Stone. That's in Ireland, I explain. This is the land of Arthur. You know, round table, knights. She nods. The official Castell Coch guide won't have any of it. Arthur has no connection whatsoever with this Castle, he announces, adding, the Marquis was a Christian, as if Arthur and God were mutually exclusive. The exchange goes over Mami's head. She thinks the building to be like those of the Samurai. Swords and lances on the walls, gilded doorways, wood-slab tables, great cooking pots, beds you can't ever imagine sleeping in. Anyone tried faking an Arthur connection? I ask the guide. It seems a reasonable question given the fact that virtually the entire edifice in which we are standing is a replica. He ignores me. You're not from around here, are you? he says to Mami, making tourist-guide conversation. No, she gives him a wide, white-toothed smile. I am from Japan.

On our way back through the trees to the car park we pass a snake of children arriving for a visit. Many of them carry plastic Excaliburs, there are a few shields, one or two sport grey polythene helmets. Just our way of keeping history alive, I explain. Mami nods.

THE GARTH

Heading north from the city this is the first real hill you come to, sitting opposite the outcrop that nestles Castell Coch. The ridge would run all the way from Llantrisant to Newport if the Taf would let it. But the river cuts deep. The western outcrop is the Garth. The Englishman who went up this hill came down a mountain. They made bits of that film here. Hugh Grant and Kenneth Griffiths carrying mud loads to the top by bucket, horse, trailer, wheelbarrow, cup, anything, just to make the hill high enough to register on the Ordnance Survey as more than it is, to make it a real mountain. All cobblers, naturally. In the film, although the hill shown is this one, the village shots were made in north Wales. Cardiff suburbs apparently are not regarded as photogenically Welsh.

On a fine day the Garth commands decent views of the city, the Bristol Channel, the Taf, Pontypridd to the north, and the outlying suburbs of Newport to the east. I last went there with a trail of party-goers celebrating my partner's fiftieth birthday. This was the designated start of a long celebratory day. A walk to begin with, to clear the head and ready the body. We'd check the air, take in the views, feel good about ourselves. As it went it was mostly mist. We all stood on top of one of the Garth's three hummocks and stared out into the fog. Hardly any point in taking a photo. This is one of three megalithic burial barrows, I announced. Giants are rumoured to be buried here. Chieftains with their jewels beside them. King Arthur and his waiting armies. Hidden wonders. The remains of UFOs crash-landed 5,000 years back. You have to say something. My audience looked bored. What's that fourth hump, over there? someone asked. An earthwork thrown up during the war. Base for a radar mast. I think they grew vegetables on its sloping sides. Nothing there now. Grass and mushrooms. Next to it was a sign put up by the local community council warning visitors not to dig among the megalithic grass. This activity had been done to death, of course, by innumerable teams of visiting archaeologists bent on establishing the great truth behind Arthur's reign. The most they ever found was a cracked pot and a charred fragment of bone. Could these three aligned hummocks actually direct Venusian spaceships to their landing grounds? Or were they the knot-end of a powerful Ley channelling magic up from Glastonbury? I found a Macdonald's wrapper at the base of the trig point. Pretty good considering the nearest outlet was the drive-in at Asda, at least twenty minutes down the path. Tidy. I picked it up and stuffed it in my pack.

In summer the Garth is the destination for many a family with their anorak-clad toddlers. It's an easy hill walk, a touch of almost-wilderness only a few minutes drive from home. Apart from one not too well camouflaged silage tower the view south bears the illusion out. Trees, green hillside, hedgerow, the remains of a ruined cottage or two. Not a road, real habitation or pylon line in sight. Horses trek across here from the local riding stables. Illegally, so do motor mountain bikers, clad like Martians and cutting the turf to make it resemble canals.

On the way down Alma tells me how it was when she saw the famous film. You couldn't hear it. We sat in front of five girls you could tell were going to make a racket. And they did. Boyfriend said this, she said that. The man next to me went to sleep, and snored. The one in front kept his eyes closed and the guy next to him spent the entire film explaining what was going on. There was a woman two rows in front I thought was being resuscitated from the way her bloke was struggling with her blouse. And two kids on the end of her row were listening to rap on their walkmans. Tickety-tick. Then someone complained about the noise and there was a performance as the attendants arrived, flashed their torches, and told people to be quiet. I would have moved but you couldn't, the place was packed. And I haven't told you about the popcorn, sweet wrappers, and coke slurping yet, nor about the man who'd brought in a bag of fish and chips under his mack. Don't worry, I tell her, the film will be on TV soon, small and quiet. Not the same, she replies.

The village stuffed between the hill's base and the inky Taf is aptly named Gwaelod y Garth, the Garth's bottom. It's almost as Welsh a place as it sounds and fervently proud of its status as not part of Cardiff city. The accent is different. That changes as you head out north through Whitchurch. Hark hark the lark does not stretch this far. I try to explain this but Alma is from Liverpool and has no idea of what I'm on about at all.

Fresh faced and ready for Brains, we drive back along the Garth's sheep-grid protected, single file blacktop, round and down the heart-stop hairpin, and back to the A470 for the brief roar along the dual carriage way to noise, party food, hark hark the slurping, and home.

LLANDAF

This is the city within a city; the village that was once two miles into the country but has now been swallowed; the high outpost of the well to do, the monied, the powerful, the crachach; an historical shambles that appears to have been here ever since records began. Llandaf. The llan, the sacred place, on the unholy Taf.

Llandaf sits on a plateau of Triassic sandstone to the north of Cardiff. Its cathedral rests in a hollow. The ancient Roman road from Caerleon to Neath, the Portway, forded the Taf here, climbing past the Cathedral to move west along what is now High Street and Ely Road. The llan itself is even earlier. Pre-Christian burials have been uncovered. St Teilo[1] built his first church of wood, wattle and white-washed boulder in this spot in AD 560. So it is said. There's little else in Cardiff, bar the Roman parts of the Castle, that can be traced back this far.

I'm approaching over the fields, the old way. I've crossed Pontcanna and Llandaf Fields and negotiated the miniature golf course facing the select apartments of The Crescent. A hundred years ago there was a stream here and a tucking mill near what's now a riding school. A tucking mill? *Tucking* means *fulling*, one of the final processes in cloth production. This involves pounding the cloth with stream-driven hammers in pits filled with a mixture of water, and fullers earth. The fibres thickened and matted together. On checking with St Fagans I found that they often added urine. It made for better felt.

The path over Western Avenue footbridge with cars by the gallon thumping below drops me into the UWIC car park, site of the ancient Llandaf corn mill. The mill pond is now Llandaf RFC club house, the yard at the back is full of weeds. The Cathedral is up ahead with the ruins of the Bishop's Palace spiking the skyline above the Cathedral School's cricket pitch to the west. Among the trees here is a half-hidden cemetery which has a stone bridge as its centrepiece. This masonry arch was designed by John Pritchard to connect what became known as the transpontine churchyard with the north burial ground. But the stream it once crossed has gone. The bridge sits there, gliding over emptiness, surreal Victoriana, some empty gin bottles and a bust bicycle beneath it, its purpose gone.

The Cathedral is the Llandaf centrepiece, of course, hidden in its hollow, hard to see behind tree and outbuilding. Grey stone, mightily ecclesiastical. And over the centuries it has suffered, oh how it has. Its first Norman Bishop, Urban, turned Teilo's tiny church into something grander at around 1107. Urban was out to impress Rome and draw power and influence to himself. Not only did he rededicate his new cathedral to St Peter but disinterred the bones of Dyfrig from Ynys Enlli and reburied them at Llandaf. By the implication of their local entombment Urban would claim Dyfrig in addition to Teilo as a Llandaf founder. As the monks washed the bones the water bubbled

as if a red hot stone had been immersed among them. Not that Urban got anywhere through his manoeuvring. He built a magnificent arch at the eastern end. The great arch is still there today. But Rome remained recalcitrant. Llandaf stayed small.

Over the centuries additions accumulated around the Norman core. Towers were built to the west and the east. Towers fell. Geoffrey of

Monmouth died here. Giraldus Cambrensis and Archbishop Baldwin preached from the cross on the Green to encourage support for the Third Crusade. St Teilo's tomb became a site of holy pilgrimage and place where solemn oaths were sworn. But, like shares, past performance is not always a sign of future growth. Llandaf fell on hard times. By time of the Reformation, following Owain Glyndwr's

thirteenth century desecrations, including the sacking of the Bishop's Palace, the disastrous Anthony Kitchen found himself appointed Bishop. Rather like an early Norman Wisdom, he proceeded to sell off church lands and dispose of the diocesan silver, arms flailing, as fast as he could. He did this not because he needed the money but because kind purchasers asked him. Kitchen, a man of many smiles, could not say no. The great wealth of Llandaf disappeared from his hands.

Further troubles occurred when the civil war struck and Cromwell's soldiers rolled in. Like the Germans in Poland they used the nave as a tavern, burned the Cathedral's books for warmth, and let their pigs trough in the font. Could there ever be such a thing as a respectful army? Cromwell demanded the Cathedral forfeit what treasures it might have left. The revered plates, cups and crosses went. An empty shell of crumbling masonry was left to weather the Cardiff rain. It did so, ivy clad and wrecked, for two centuries until the Victorians, under Bruce Knight, the first Dean to be appointed since Norman times, began to rebuild. His successor, Dean Connybeare employed John Pritchard and Cathedral rehabilitation soared – new slates, new everything – a new front, new spire, new nave.

It took the Germans one night in 1941 to put a landmine through the roof and reduce the building once more to a rain drenched shell. But on this occasion reconstruction was swifter. It took twenty years and was complete by 1960. Watertight, ancient, modern, a meld of fragments. George Pace's parabolic concrete arch is surmounted by a cylindrical organ case carrying Jacob Epstein's enormous unpolished aluminium 'Christ in Majesty'. Go round the sides and you'll see this awe-inspiring idol weakened by the addition of niches filled with gold-painted nick-knackery[2], like some suburban front-room.

This is the problem with Cardiff's claim to religious significance. The Cathedral's interior, barring the Epstein, lacks grace, lacks grandeur. It is a sprawling mix of styles and finishes: unfashionable regimental banners hanging into twelfth-century space; polished wood memorials abutting black and white snaps of HMS Llandaf at war; a shambling shop selling the worst of religioso trivia: prayer place mats, Jesus pencil sharpeners, Celtic cross earrings. Seventeenth-century fine-chiselled letter work is upstaged by garish twentieth century painted additions. St Teilo is being gaudily regilded. St Dyfrig's head is cracked. There's a sign telling me this is him. Venerated for nearly a millennium and a half and now celebrated in nothing more elaborate than Stephen's Ink on cardboard. This is Cathedral as junk shop. It needs a strong hand and a large store-room. History and religion mix well but here they're simply holding each other back.

Outside, up the Dean's Steps, on the Green stands the tenth-century preaching cross. Only the lower third of the shaft and the stone into which it is set are original. Round the corner is St Teilo's well according to all the records possessed of miraculous healing powers, a venerated place of supplication and sacrifice for more than thirteen hundred years. Llans and holy wells have a natural and usually pagan affinity. To find this one I ask directions of a cherub-faced ancient laying out Easter hymnals along the pews. It's in the wall of my cottage, he smiles. Floods like something else come winter. You should see it. Does it cure anything, I enquire? No. It's just a spring. There are lots of them in Llandaf. It's there, behind its iron grating. Murky. A cigarette packet floating on its surface. No abandoned crutches line the pavement. No discarded bandages. No one selling souvenir bottles of holy well water. Is this opportunity lost or Protestant reticence? Who knows. The city shows its age. Space and slowness. The Chinese restaurant on the corner is a subdued intrusion. Only the cars, parked in an expected urban sprawl, prevent the space from feeling older.

I take the lower path beside the Arls field towards the Taf weir. This is Ffordd y Meirw, the Road of the Dead, the route by which corpses were brought from Whitchurch before that place had a burial ground of its own. Llandaf is high on its ridge beside me. The path wends through quiet, deserted woods until quite suddenly it climbs up to the vast watery spread that is Llandaf Weir. Amid the floating river debris scullers streak out from the Cardiff Rowing Club. The place has an utterly unexploited Edwardian air, ignored by event entrepreneurs trying to turn a quick pound. But there's a new tarmac path going in. Watch this space.

I'm using the 1880 OS two-and-half inch to guide me and surprisingly it still works. The flotchet, the mill stream sluice, is gone but the tracks leading to it are all still in place. To my left the map shows a spring. The path I climb to take me back up to Llandaf Road is appropriately running wet. I emerge just north of the perfectly named Cathedral City pub, the Mitre. In the late 60s I brought George MacBeth here when he wanted to escape the false camaraderie and hustle of a Poet's Conference being held in Cardiff's Central Hotel. Why we came here I don't recall. But it was out of town. George had yet to take up with Lisa St Aubin de Teran and reach his zenith as a poet with a foot in the camps of both the traditionalists and the moderns. He was a Scot, although you could hardly tell that from his accent, with a taste for the celtic worlds. We drank bitter slowly until a dope-driven local partisan picked what turned out to be a ferocious argument about what it was that constituted verse. This stuff, shouted our antagonist, waving the copy of George's book I'd shown him, is nothing like Wordsworth. A surprisingly accurate observation but delivered with emotion rather than tranquillity. As happens all too often when poets drink together, and in particular to me, and despite not being in the wrong, we were asked to leave. We walked up the road to the Heathcock where our presence turned out to be no more acceptable. The Llandaf telegraph was working well. They wouldn't let us in. George's experiments in verse involved word patterns drawn from, among other things, the arrival of the panda Chi-Chi in Moscow and a vowel analysis of the work of the German author, Friederike Mayröcker. "Oi o ua : aui ie aeie : u aee e ; oe o," chanted George at the burly barman[3]. The telegraph obviously didn't reach the mock-timbered Black Lion, at the bottom end of Llandaf High Street. No one said a thing when we went in.

Back where I started, in the UWIC car park, someone has stuffed a double-glazing flyer behind my windscreen wiper. There's an artic broken down on the Avenue and the traffic is backing up beyond the junction at William Clarke's monumental masoners. Llandaf always was a well-trafficked crossroads. Romans from the west, roundheads from the south. Pilgrims from all directions. I've checked Macbeth's posthumous collected to see if he ever recorded anything about his visit. He did not.

Things That Went Missing
When Bishop Holgate
Was In Charge

A cope and vestments
A crock
A brass cauldron
Three iron bars
for fastening the great door
A sliver model of St Teilo's shoes
Two silver mitres
Some silver apostles
A cross of gilded silver
A gilded brass image of the virgin
The silver head of St Dyfrig
The arms of St Dyfrig
Twelve silver bells
Two great silver candlesticks
A silver gilt chalice
Four silver cruets
Two silver basins
A flat pax with cover gilded
Two silver pyxies
A gilded maser
Two silver gilt sensers
A silver ship to carry frankincense
Numerous girdles
Many bedes
Four chains weighing 30 ozs
The pontifical gold ring
A chasuble of tinsel
St Teilo's head of silver-gilt
The head of St Euddogwy in silver
Two basons of silver
The silver-gilt shrine of St Teilo
One arm of St Dyfrig composition unknown
The Book of Teilo with on its rear boards
affixed to it in half relief a man
of youthful countenance
with one hand raised.

[articles from the wealth of Llandaf
which vanished during the years
of Holgate's bishopric, mid seventeenth
century. Suspected of taking for his
own use. Always said this wasn't so.]

THE PINEAPPLE

I've just returned fifty-two empty flagons to the Pineapple. Forty-three of these have been rejected as being either damaged or from the wrong brewery. I have managed four and six and have ordered myself a pint of Hancocks. The unwanted bottles are left in a sack in the street outside. This is the early seventies before plastic took over the world and when beer came in two-pint glass bottles rather than small metal cans. When it was beer too. I scratch the start of a poem on the back of a beer mat. This is a break from editing my magazine. Early evening, sun slanting through the trees, clear air. At such times I have traditionally drawn the curtains. I'm the Bard of Llandaf North. At least sometimes I think I am.

Llandaf North is a small working-class Cardiff suburb on the wrong side of the tracks from Whitchurch. A dozen or so streets of terraced housing, church, school, set of pubs, the long green of Hailey Park separating accommodation from the Taf. To the north, beyond the allotments and the outpost of the Corporation rubbish dump lie the Melingriffith Tin Plate Works. Even in the 60s the plant had run out of industrial steam. But in its late-nineteenth-century hey day the Melingriffith was the jewel in Cardiff's crown – twelve mills on one site putting out 10,000 tonnes of sheet iron and 100,000 boxes of tinplate annually. Steel killed it. But it took a long time.

The stretch of land running from the back of the Cow and Snuffers was once called Llandaf Yard. This was the site of the Eagle Iron and Brass Foundry and the Glamorgan Canal unloading depot. It was stacked with coal, pig feed, timber, iron. The stuff would come in by slow barge from Merthyr, from Aberdare, and be unloaded here prior to local distribution. The canal paralleled the river, skirting Forest Farm to run through Gabalfa, down the grounds of the much fought over Welsh-medium secondary school, and on south to enter the city near Blackweir. Only the Forest Farm section now remains, the rest has been drained, converted to highway or built upon. The Llandaf Yard section has Maplewood Avenue cutting through its centre. My flat was in a hollow here: home of my literary journal, *second aeon*, my thousand volume collection of small mags, my beat novels, my concrete poetry, my cultural universe. Maplewood Court. Low rise. Common hallways. Interlopers. Disputes. Dust. Graffiti. But bearable enough.

I am in the Pineapple because it's near. I prefer the Snuffers, where Disraeli slept on his way to visit the widow Mary Ann Lewis at Greenmeadow. But after the Japanese incident once again I am no longer welcome. What is it with poets and landlords? The poet Gavin Bantock, visiting with three monoglot blue-jeaned students wanted to experience traditional Welsh life. I suggested a Sunday lunch-time half of dark and a bag of crisps. It's what we traditionally do. At the Snuffers the landlord, riding some ancient wartime anti-Nippon phantom, refused admission. These people are improperly dressed, (they wore jeans and sweatshirts, identical, like American ivy leaguers), they can't come in. Bantock tried reason: Where they come from they live in houses made of paper. How can they know of these things? It sounded so convincing. No dice. I tried appealing to the man's business sense. We want five pints. No deal. I'll put this outrage in a poem, I told him. The ultimate threat. But meaningless outside the *second aeon* subscription list. You do what you want mate. Out. I turned and accidentally knocked over a chair. Entranced and imaging this to be also a Welsh Sunday custom the Japanese did the same thing. Four upholstered chairs lay in a bar room sprawl. Bantock added a table. The Landlord moved from behind the bar with incredible swiftness. But we move quicker. Gone.

I edit by attrition. The stacks of incoming hopelessness lie in the hallway. I take a batch at a time and slowly wear myself down. Most of it rhymes badly. That which doesn't sprawls like a frying egg. The soul seems to be top subject. Pain. Darkness. Making a poem out of what the author is feeling seems, for the author anyway, to turn on the lights. The world is full of verbiage masquerading as verse. I am still at the honourable stage where I read everything submitted. I am a public service, like the BBC. It will be later, around the time of *second aeon* *#8*, that the unsolicited contributions will rise by a factor of ten. I will then start to listen to Ben Johnson, throw stuff back with hardly a look, realising that one doesn't need to eat the whole ox just to tell the quality of the meat.

In the bar I have abandoned the new poem on the beer mat and now shuffle small stacks of typescripts like cards. None of these chancers have apparently ever seen *second aeon*. Their work radiates traditionalism. Their bad rhymes echo the Lakelanders, Tennyson, Hardy, Kipling, the palpable authority of the King James translation. Not one of these parlour poets has ever heard of Pound, Eliot, Williams, Stein, let alone beat modernist concrete Liverpool pop expressionist left-handed new age post-Blakean revolution. Why should I bother? I stuff the dreadful things, full of gulls wings, patina, shards, and shopping trolleys, back into their saes[4] and draw on the brown half still sitting before me. Out of the corner of an eye I can see Frank, the part-time barman and local sonneteer, fiddling with a foolscap file. Any second now. I knock the beer into the back of my throat in one long drown and just as Frank withdraws a sheet covered with scrawl manage to slip back out through the door. What's in front of me at the flat? Sort three hundred little mags and a torrent of small, slim, self-published verse volumes into alphabetical order, stuff fifty or so sorry-not-this-time slips into brown poem-fat envelopes and then chip away at my own work.

I walk back up the avenue. The investiture party here had the whole neighbourhood hanging union flags in their windows, a beer stall in the square, and a bad band on the back of a lorry. I put a Ddraig Goch out of my front window and went to bed. I get in and the phone rings. I stand next to my giant concrete mobile an eight-foot tall assemblage of globes and rods, looking like an atomic structure, mounted on the turntable of an old Dansette record player adjusted to turn at 6 rpm (I simply increased the size of the drive wheel and added extra weights). The globes and rods are strewn with words. The poem forms and reforms before the reader as it slowly spins. It was once taken to the BBC by pantechnicon for inclusion in a John Ormond arts extravaganza. I sat with great anticipation through forty-five minutes of gabble about Welsh opera and the music of Alun Hodinott before my masterwork appeared spinning in black and white, behind the rolling final credits. Ten quid.

On the phone is a distraught contributor. Or a drunk contributor. I am uncertain. He wants to change the wording of a poem I am certain I threw on the floor at the Pineapple. He has woken with great inspiration and needs to pass the god-given gift onwards. He is Moses of Surbiton, or St Mellons, or most probably Swindon. Most of my unsolicited contributors seem to come from middle-England. I can't seem to trace your work, I offer. Are you a subscriber? No. I don't subscribe. I write. I never read anything by anyone else for fear of contamination. My work is pure. It pours from above. Listen to this. The voice, small, nasal, like a dentist's drill, spikes outwards from the earpiece. I lay the phone on the floor. It will make a noise for a while and then eventually it will stop. I put John Lee Hooker on the player. *Stutterin Blues*. The small garden and driveway visible from my window once echoed to the sound of hot metal being beaten. I pull Mary Elen Solt's *Anthology of Concrete Poetry* down from the rack and study how it can be. On the floor the small rhyming voice shows no signs of slowing, oblivious to the rest of the world.

THE TWMPATH

In a field at the top end of a blind lane running east from Rhiwbina Hill and up beyond the clattering Nant Cwmnofydd the ground rises sharply to form the Twmpath. In Welsh *twmpath* means tump. The mound might have been on the way to somewhere once but, with the roaring of Eastern Avenue to its north and the neat suburbanity of Clos Y Bryn and Brynteg beyond it to the west, it has now lost its dominance. Coming here on a bright spring day with the sun turning the fields wet green and the wooded Wenallt rising beyond the place feels like the end of the city. The motte may well have been just that. An outpost. A Norman fort, part of the Morganstown, Castell Coch, Morgraig run along the Llantrisant ridge. It's thirty foot tall, completely overgrown with holly, broom and beech, but with a flat disc of grass in its centre. Its fringes are muddy and sunken. There could have been a bailey ditch here but nine-hundred years of Welsh mist, thunder and Cardiff Rhiwbina downpour have filled it in. Climbing to the top the sound of spring birds is mixed with distant house alarms. Twitter, woop. There's youth detritus, as expected, lager cans, patch of burned grass, tree bark scuffed.

This was once Ynys-yr-Ysgallenfraith farm and the earthwork on it was long thought to be the burial mound of a Welsh chieftain. Iestyn ap Gwrgan, Lord of Glamorgan, was killed in battle against the Normans around 1089. His body, together with his horses and their trappings were buried here. So the legend goes. A spell was cast to keep the tomb from desecration. For nine hundred years it worked. In the mid-nineteenth century, emboldened by the industrial age, the tumulus was excavated, opened right to its centre. There was found "black peaty matter, excessively offensive, about two feet in depth; in this there was something like a piece of iron. The grass and broom on the original surface of the ground were quite green at first, but were discoloured upon being exposed to air."⁵ F. Fox, Esq., amateur archaeologist and in charge of the dig, tells us little else. There is no record of samples of this mysterious piece of iron being taken and if he made drawings then by now they are lost. Did Fox suffer sleepless nights as the spell caught his throat and stuffed his soul with fear? Did he die mysteriously? We do not know.

The views from the Twmpath are expectedly terrific. In its long life as farmland Rhiwbina (hill of pines) threw up many an important Welshman including Cadifor, the eleventh century Lord of Dyfed and Ifor Hael, patron of the poet Dafydd ap Gwilym. It's nice to find a Cardiff somewhere with a Welsh history. Not that the Cymry have maintained their influence. The street names around here may well be among the Welshest in the city but the local accent bears little trace of the stretched Cardiff vowel. Letters to the *Echo* protesting about bilingualism, the expansion of Welsh-medium education, and the Assembly being too nationalist usually emanate from here.

Running back from the Twmpath, below the great Mormon Church at the corner of Heol Llanishen Fach, with its perfect needle point spire taking the eye to heaven and its frontage like a fire station, lies Rhiwbina Garden Village. Or at least that part of it they managed to build. The Village, a mightily worthy experiment in co-operative ownership and community reform, was to have run to three hundred homes. The diligent lower middle classes were the target owners. The houses would be crossed by straight main roads and connected by gently curving side-streets. There would be grass and softening woodland, sundials, clocks, balconies, buff-coloured cottages, red-tiled roofs, room for breath. Space to clear the enclogged mind. In the event the Great War, the Depression and failure of the group leader's nerve[6] contributed to only seventy or so steeply pantiled residences being built at the back of Rhiwbina Station. The diligent lower middle classes failed to arrive. They put in a bank and added a community hall for the local amateur players, the Bridge Club and the pensioners. Prices went up. You only moved here if your job didn't make your hands dirty. In the 1980s they opened an Indian. There's a Spar. You can walk to the shops with your terrier in utter safety. I go back down the hill. One pensioner leaning on a gatepost. Someone delivering a new settee. Birdbath in a front garden. Still no pub.

THE JUNCTION TERRACE COOKING MOUND

Some sites remain forever elusive. In the CADW guidebook the Iron Age Cooking Site listed as a short way along a public path in woodland to the south of Junction Terrace in Radyr sounded promising. Cooking mounds were the residue which remained after our woad-smeared iron age ancestors had completed making edible the day's kill. The method was to heat great stones over a fire and then plunge them into water in order to heat it. The mounds were a mouldering heap of discarded stone, charcoal and gnawed bone. The one in the Junction Terrace woods was described as rather shapeless and roughly oval, and then, tellingly, "now landscaped into an amenity area". We wandered among the alders and birch, the ivy-clad oaks and the thick shrub growing along the banks of the stream. Neat benches, half a bike, a deflated plastic football wedged in a tree trunk. No mound[7]. A rise in the ground near the picnic area turns out to be moss-covered hardcore dumped here before the war.

Back in Junction Terrace middle-aged men in training pants and sports sweats are mowing their lawns. A youth in an oil-stained T has his head under the bonnet of a VW Golf. A couple of four-year-olds play with Lego on a doorstep. Out front, where the great shunting yards used to be, is urban desolation. The coal is finished, industry has moved on. I ask a neatly-dressed pensioner with a Scottie on a lead if she knows where the cooking mound might be. She shakes her head and looks at me as if I were mad. Soon a new housing estate will go up and the unseemly silence of bird call and air through tree top will vanish. Made to fit the world's new circumstance, like the mound.

It's the same problem a mile north in the woods above the Ty Nant. Here I am hunting the Lesser Garth Cave. The Lesser Garth is, as you might work out from its name, a smaller version of the Neolithic tomb topped Greater Garth hill to its north. The Lesser Garth is mostly eaten away by quarry working, its dolomite stone blasted, hacked, crushed and ripped. What's left rises steeply up from Morganstown for 590 feet through thick beech wood. Next to the road are allotments full of runner beans, plastic bags billowing on poles, potatoes, cauliflower, cabbages, bird-scare windmills, and shabby huts inside which men in stained shirts and mud-caked trousers drink tea from flasks and smoke.

Somewhere above this is the cave in which bronze age burials were found, pottery shards, crucibles, bronze, iron and silver slivers and the bones of animals. Cavers record the system as having a main chamber 100 yards long and 50 feet high. Huge. But I can't find it. The beech mast slides beneath my feet. Saplings crack as I haul myself through. There's a sheet of rusty corrugated iron from fifty years ago, a wood frame from the bottom of a packing case but nothing else that isn't natural. No cans. No plastic. No detritus. So near the city it doesn't seem real. One of the beech trees has an initial carved into it but so long ago that it's illegible. I slide back down to the car. Is it worth asking about this among the family diners the pub? Probably not.

After two failures the chance discovery of Gelynis Pick Your Own Farm and Vineyard, stuffed between the M4 and the Taf, is brilliant recompense. The farmhouse dates from 1570, erected originally as a dwelling for Hugh Lambert, iron master, who moved here from Kent to exploit the Garth and Pentyrch deposits. The mullioned windows and mortared-stone walls are a testament to the building's longevity, more ancient than most places still standing in Cardiff. Grade II listed. At first glance it looks as if it should do better than that. As a farm Gelynis has market gardened for decades. Today it offers honey, beans, soft fruit, strawberries grow-bag grown on trestles with the fruits pickably trailing at hand height, sweetcorn, pumpkins, flowers, and hanging baskets. The land traps the sun, glows green, is hemmed by a triangle of roaring motorway, river, and the main valley rail line out of Cardiff. The Taf Trail runs on its eastern side. You enter over a level crossing: gates, bells, notices and warning lights. There's an emergency phone prominently fixed on a purpose installed pole. It seems impossible that this place can remain rural, but it does.

Beyond the farmhouse lies a rowing boat full of bedding plants and a buckled corrugated shed. Rust and rain have done it. Beneath the weeds and the collapsed and tangled roof are the wrecked remains of a plough and a harrow. Behind, across a narrow field and facing the barn, is a doorless garage with no track leading to it. Inside is a mouldering Hillman. A path bends behind the farmhouse to reach a single user black iron bridge across the river. The bridge carries a fat water pipe destined for Barry. This was originally the Pentyrch to Forest Halt Light Railway river bridge carrying coal and iron to the tin plate works at Melingriffith. Today leisure cyclists in hard-shell plastic hats and lycra one-piece suits cross on their days-out, peddling north. From the bridge's centre you can see Castell Coch with the Taf running straight from it. Below me there's a Tesco trolley resting on the bottom. Not deep. On a fishing platform sits a rod-less glue-sniffer who alternates between blowing a mouth organ and raving at the water drifting past.

We leave with three kilo of broad beans (paid for) and at least eight strawberries apiece, consumed before we reached the till. That's okay, says the owner, if you eat too many the trains'll get you on the crossing. The Ddraig Goch flutters on a flag pole. A pair of pensioners drink tea in Gelynis's open air café. A four-car sprinter rattles south along the track, full of shoppers from Ponty. Artics roar on the M4. There's just too much transport going on here. Gelynis belongs to another age. It shouldn't still be here. But it is.

THE COMMON AT WHITCHURCH

When you reach Whitchurch Common from the south you expect to find a green lung surrounded by cottages; something old with oaks at its fringes and a maypole; but this is Wales and this is Cardiff so there's nothing like that. The Common – Gwaun Treoda – is a badly-formed egg shape, criss-crossed by roads and dotted with outbuildings, including an upholster's works, and on a rise on the north east side, Ararat, a Baptist chapel. There's no circuit, no boundary dog amble or path for walkers or runners which doesn't make itself cross the blistering A4054 road to Merthyr at least twice.

The common has been here since the times of the medieval manors when Whitchurch was entirely a village and Cardiff a town miles away across Mynydd Bychan, the Great Heath. In the late twentieth century John Tripp lived here, with his blacksmith father, in a bungalow to the back of Ararat. You'd meet him, occasionally, wearing a suede jacket that he'd lifted from an admirer, taking his notebook and his browsing self to the Plough or the Maltsters where he'd scratch a draft or two then lose himself in the fog of beer that generally filled his afternoons. Tripp was a fervent Nationalist and a long-term supporter of the Welsh deciding their own destiny on their side of Offa's Dyke. His father, however, took a different view. On days when I went to the bungalow to collect JT's contributions for *second aeon* (he wrote the literary reviews) I would often be confronted with the incongruity of Coronation plates displayed across the living room wall and portraits of Her Majesty in small frames in the hall. The Bungalow resembled the bedsit in Tony Hancock's *Sunday Afternoon*. A fifties style disarray of strewn newspapers, a cigarette smouldering in heavy glass ashtray, socks in the armchairs, a half-drunk bottle of Sandyman's Port on the mantle-shelf, a crossword, incomplete, on the table. On one famous occasion – Empire Day, Commonwealth Day, the Queen's Birthday, something like that – Paul Tripp, retired, had hoisted the Union Jack on a small flagpole rigged in the Bungalow's front garden. He was an unbending traditionalist. JT stoically stood grimacing in the lounge.

Tripp was a celebrator of Cardiff. His small book from the early seventies, *Bute Park and other Poems*, had verse set in various Cardiff locations with photos of the poet visiting the same spots to illustrate the text. The Castle, the Station, the nightclubs, the city centre's pubs, are all here. There's a shot of Tripp looking young and tough at the Lake with the Captain Scott memorial lighthouse in the background (clocktower, no lights, small door to gain entrance, access by boat, Tripp claimed to want to live there, for the peace in order to write). But there's little about Whitchurch. A short poem about a funeral at Pantmawr and a piece about the library. Nothing closer to home.

At the west end of the Common where the Whitchurch Brook takes a right turn before vanishing south the locals once kept pigs. Whitchurch water got so polluted that council inspectors were sent to confiscate the offending animals. Whenever they showed, however, the sties were always empty. No, no pigs here. But you could smell them. Hogs were hidden under beds, sows were camouflaged with rugs. A bunch were herded into the chapel vestry where god protected their rights. The vicar ate bacon for months.

When JT died in 1986 – suddenly, young, mid-fifties and still writing like fury – a local group proposed and erected a memorial bench. It sat on the path to the West of Ararat, a wooden affair with an engraved plaque. JT, Whitchurch's greatest bard, could just as well have been a rose grower or a scout master. Whitchurch has a bookshop now, cross the Brook and head up Merthyr Road, past what used to be known as Millward's Terrace (now 87-111 Merthyr Road), beyond the Tabernacle Presbyterian Church and into the Lower Village. Can you buy John Tripp's books there? What do you think?

notes

1. Teilo is still here. According to a 1736 record builders working on the cathedral during one of its innumerable restorations found the saint's coffin, opened it and saw the corpse, wrapped in leather, with his pastoral staff, pewter cross and chalice lying tightly by his side. The coffin has since been lost but the saint's skull, held upright by some gilded apparatus, is in the Cathedral's possession. Carbon dating shows this to be genuine thirteenth century. Unfortunately Teilo lived in the seventh.
2. These include figures of angels playing musical instruments and other box-wood carvings salvaged from the stalls after the 1941 destruction, now gilded and wasted where they are.
3. This was in perfect echo of George Melly's famous riposte when set upon by a bunch of muggers. Rather than hand over his wallet he stood his ground and began reciting Kurt Schwitters' early dada masterpiece, 'The Ursonata'. Melly's attackers thought him to be mad and fled.
4. SAEs – Stamped Addressed Envelopes – essential for the return of unsolicited contributions. Fire your work off – even today – without one of these and all you'll get will be silence.
5. Proceeding of the Cambrian Archaeological Association at Cardiff in 1849.
6. H. Stanley Jervons, holder of the Chair in Economics at University College, Cardiff. Left for Allahabad in 1913.
7. Once it's pointed out to you, as it was done for me on a later visit, the Mound is actually obvious. Enter the woodland from the north and the Mound, a ten meter piece of grassed over landscaping is on your right.

SOUTH

BUTE STREET

Bute Street is slowing down. The chicanes, narrows and parking bays of urban traffic calming have made their appearance along its length. The render on the Queen Street-Butetown rail link embankment retaining wall has been chipped back to reveal clean Victorian stone.

Before the railways this was mostly tide-field meadow, marshland, drainage ditches, fishing henges, the Cardiff south moors – Soudrey. No one lived here much until Bute drained it for his great docklands. Calling it Tiger Bay came later. Portuguese seamen reputedly sailing though the rough waters of the Bristol Channel said reaching Cardiff was like sailing into a bay of Tigers. Did they? Who knows. The name rose, stuck, then, when they pulled the old streets down to replace them with high rise, fell. There's the Tiger Bay Café on the bright new frontage and they are planning a Tiger Bay Bar for the new Millennium Centre but the name is not much on the lips of the locals. This is Butetown. Was, is, still.

Butetown is now an increasingly Muslim district. The sprawling two-up two-down, back to back bad housing to the west was replaced in the fifties with new brick link and high-rise. These are already worn to the wire and are again being replaced. Turn left at Hannah Street and there's a mosque. Further up near Maria Street is the Greek Orthodox. But hardly anyone attends now. The Loudon Square, upper Butetown population has a high proportion of Arab, Somali and Afro-Caribbean with a smattering of Bengali. Three women pass wearing full veils, a big man jogs with his track-suit hood pulled right up. Three black kids cycle down the pavement on bikes they've long

outgrown.

At the north end are the twin towers of the Church of St Mary the Virgin and St Stephen the Martyr. This celebration of Christ is the replacement for Cardiff's lost and sunk original, the first St Mary's Church which stood on St Mary's Street when that road bordered the Taf. After the flood of 1607 the great church entered a period of terminal decline. Its replacement, erected with cash from the Marquis of Bute and funds raised by, among others, William Wordsworth, opened on the new site to fanfare and flags in 1843. There was a fete in progress when I passed it during a blazing afternoon in August, 2000. The stall holders were wilting. Two or three decorator's tables were covered with car boot junk, a fat lady in a hat was running a cake stall which also sold crisps and cans of coke. There was a spot where  you could throw darts at cards, and, next to it, a table loaded with bin bags, plastic clothes pegs and washing bowls. Someone had resurrected, from a basement, one of those zigzag wires connected to a bell where the object is get a wooden handled hook to traverse the course without making anything ring. But there was no battery, so it didn't work. House music thrummed from two huge speakers set in the Church porch. There were at least half a dozen stall holders, smoking, smiling and talking, but not a single punter, anywhere. This was three o'clock on a Saturday. Next door ran the cut grass of a medium sized playing field, goal posts at each end, no dumped cars or other wreckage. Empty. In all the thousands of times I've passed it I've never seen anyone there.

Further up towards Bute Square (now renamed Callaghan Square after one of Cardiff's greatest political sons) lay the site of the legendary Charleston Club. This was a forties-style drink and gambling joint complete with a bow-tied doorman. Charles took your coat and directed you to either smoky roulette or soft, hip, modern jazz. The clientele were largely media types, a few writers, the odd actor, and the occasional administrator. Most of these guys simply fancied a drink after ten thirty in the stumbling city once everything else had shut down. This was the early seventies and lifestyles in Cardiff had yet to make their significant hedonistic shift.

Today clubs dominate the city centre, south to the Hayes, north up Park Place. Finding somewhere to drink is no longer a Cardiff worry. next to the Charleston's site a bright new Salvation Army development which looks like a Dan Dare vision of future housing. The diesel rattles gently along the embankment top on its regular shuttle. First car empty, three stragglers in the second. There's a bunch of dust from a passing lorry. A few tourists fluttering their guide books head south on foot. Clean trainers. Bright faces. Not far. Ahead green and orange glass art works dominate the square on the bay side of the rail line. The city is trying hard to move south.

LLOYD GEORGE AVENUE

A pin-eyed zoom-head in a check shirt driving a McNiff van takes the polish from the back of my left shoe. I'm turning off Tyndall Street towards Lloyd George Avenue. It's sheeting rain, a grey slash coming up the boulevard from the south. The wind is slamming the velcro of my anorak collar into my reddening face. Cardiff weather. I round the corner by Edward England Ltd – *1842 Potato Merchants for 150 years* – flogging bagged Maris Piper from their stone built warehouse. Their car park is marked out in new white stripes to be sold to city centre day shoppers. The site is placed well enough. It's at the interface between the bay and the town, the barrier the planners want to see dissolve like a set of A&E stitches. Nothing is completely finished when I visit. Dug up tarmac, patched pavement, loose brick, sand, JCBs doing 40 down the dual carriage way, guys in hard hats. But when it's done it'll flow like an airport runway directly to Pier Head Building, that Big Ben symbol of Wales' parliament, red brick focus of the nation – clock, history, weather vane, future – all in one.

The Avenue runs parallel to the site of the former Bute West Dock the break for maritime fortune made by the second Marquis of Bute in around 1839. This is where Cardiff first began to stretch its economic muscle. Exporting Dowlais iron from the town quay in Westgate Street wasn't enough. How could it be? King coal was arriving. Like a nineteenth-century Bill Gates the Marquis made his early move, established the operating system, and took over the city. Docks and the land they're dug into. Own both and you control the world.

When the second Marquis got to it, the land here – the great East Moors – was nothing but salt marsh and fog. "A direful swamp over which the spring tides flowed, leaving dangerous dykes, swamps and gullies" (Wm Rees – *Cardiff – A History of the City*). Everything south of the end of present day St Mary Street was open field. Cows grazed and were brought to be milked roughly where the Mill Lane sex shop currently stands. Land drains were installed, a sea wall was erected, a deep cut made out to the Bristol Channel through the silky, clinging mud. The godwit, the sandpiper, the plover moved south. Give them another 160 years and they'd be moved again.

As the industrial revolution roared through the western world Cardiff's time arrived. On the back of iron and steel, coal exports rose exponentially. New docks were created – bigger, better, deeper Bute East Dock, Roath Dock, Roath Basin, Queen Alexandra.

Shipowners set up shop. By 1880 the city was host to more than ninety companies including Blue Jacket, White Jacket, Evan-Thomas Radcliffe, the Cardiff Steam Navigation Company and John Cory. Local population exploded. Cheap workers' terraced housing spread out from the city centre like a glowing stain.

But revolutions fade, and in Cardiff today, as far as heavy industry goes, the paleness is palpable. The Bute West Dock is filled-in and covered with brick and glass apartments. No private gardens, no sheds, no place to store your muddy boots. £250,000 for three rooms of ash, silver, multi-sink and panoramic view. Rigarossa, Atlantic Wharf, Mallards Reach, Hightower, Adventurers Quay, Millennium Waterfront, Scott Harbour. Wonderfully pronounceable names, saleable as addresses to the never-Welsh, non-Welsh and the anti-Welsh and with hardly a lexical connection to the land they occupy between them. The dock feeder goes through here. Like a canal through a wet Venice. Beautiful, impractical, its original purpose forever gone.

When the idea for the great link between the Bay development and the city was first mooted by Cardiff Bay Development Corporation the connecting highway was designated Bute Avenue. It would have a hi-tech tramway running parallel to it. The old Taf Vale rail link between Queen Street Station and Bute Road was to be no more. But money and politics intervened. The rail link – frequent and cheap – terminates at the renamed Cardiff Bay station. It's separated from Lloyd George Avenue by heavy urban planting and a barbed wire intruder fence. On the far side is the real Butetown. Does the fence protect the residents there from death by diesel two-car? Or does it

just keep them out? The City and County of Cardiff – CBDC's successors – gave the Avenue its new name. Lloyd George – Welsh, proud, redolent of high point history and achievement. At the opening ceremony the Labour council failed to invite a single Liberal. This was politics. Lloyd George would have understood.

Through the unending rain I go down it. Leaves. Hoardings painted by local schools, you have to keep the community happy. Graffiti already on the Letton underpass. No Macdonald's wrappers. Lots of street furniture. Bunch of joggers in streaming kit. At the bottom is a chrome tower and fountain telling us that this really is the future. Water cascades across its surface and gets blown off in sheeting streams. This is Wales, after all. There's a gull parked on top.

MOUNT STUART SQUARE

Coming to this Square can be a bit of a disappointment. If you were expecting a large, spacious courtyard on the Edinburgh or Dublin model then forget it. Mount Stuart is not open. Its roadway describes a squat rectangle. At its midpoint is the creaky five storey stone pile of the Cardiff Coal Exchange. This place was once the centre of the city's commercial life. There's a blue plaque, unreadably high, above the main door to mark the fact. But there's not a gram of coal exchanged there now. The last sack left Cardiff in the sixties. We import now. Ahead of me are a group of giggling Asians, headscarves, dangling gold, trainers, screaming bright socks. They're heading for the Dowlais arcade that leads past the massage parlour to the flats of West Bute Street. We are in cosmopolitan country. I round the corner where the old buildings have all gone for redevelopment and take in the spiky frame of the Millennium Stadium on the skyline beyond.

Mount Stuart Square, named after Lord Mountstuart, the Napoleonic period MP for Cardiff and heir to the Bute estate, was where Cardiff's wealth once circulated. You can tell by the shape and weight of the buildings. Put up at the end of the nineteenth century when coal, iron and steel were making the city spin, they exude power – Cambrian Buildings, Empire House, Perch Buildings, Beynon House, Crichton House – home of the Capital and Counties Bank, Baltic House, Phoenix Buildings. The centrepiece, the once-mighty Coal Exchange, which in 1886 had more than 1,500 members running around in hats, spats and cigars, now moulders. A local promoter, Red Kite, puts on concerts. Van Morrison, amazingly, played here recently with Linda Gail Lewis and a Welsh pick-up band, turning out the sort of bar room rock and roll that Cardiffians favour. Back in the eighties I saw the Five Blind Boys of Alabama bring the house down with contagious gospel sung to a mainly black audience of large women in their Sunday best. But for most of the time, until redevelopment takes hold, and smart office refurb, and ready conference facility come back on stream, the building sleeps. The tired leviathan. Old newspapers blow across its frontage. Rain dirt collects on its window sills. This used to be Cardiff Bay Development Corporation territory, before it was disbanded and its powers transferred to the City, CBDC embossed waste-bins are everywhere. The City's first action as successor was to suggest renaming the whole area something like Cardiff South. Thank the Lord and Muddy Waters that idea got shot down.

Today the Square houses a mix of arts agencies, a few charities, media companies, design studios, and PR manipulators. Harry Holland, probably Cardiff's best-known painter, has a studio here and one of the pubs has become a gourmet restaurant. The Square has changed its nature but it has not slid back.

The western edge once housed the chapel which later became the notorious Casablanca, the first and best of the city's stoned-sixties night clubs. You came here if you were strong. It's new

apartments now. The Square, of course, is surrounded on all sides by mainstream, classic-mode Butetown. This is pre-Bay development Cardiff dockland, or at least, what's left of it. To the north are the mesh of new streets built to replace the mesh of old streets running up to Loudon Square. That, with its classic Victoriana, they pulled down. South is James Street and a further slice of local housing that separates Mount Stuart from Techniquest, Harry Ramsden's and the water beyond. The plan for Cardiff Bay is based, largely, on Baltimore. Fleets of councillors, developers and other local worthies were flown over year on year to see how it was done. "Urban renewal equals Negro removal", black American author James Baldwin was quoted at them, using heavy irony. But not in Caerdydd, brother. Not yet.

Walking out of the Square at the south end I pass the White Hart and the empty shop from which, ten years back, the short-lived Bay FM, Cardiff's only rap station, ran. I turn into the thin splinter of a recreation ground, built along the line of the old Glamorgan Canal, that runs from the Royal Hamadryad Hospital near the waterfront, skirting Loudon Square and central Butetown to the main London-Fishguard railway to the north. At the James Street intersection there are some planted shrubs and a this-wonderful-park-is-here-for-the-people-of-Butetown artist-carved entrance gates but after that it's worn grass, smashed divans, wrecked washing machines and litter. The blind backs of Mount Stuart's buildings have been elaborately spray painted. 'Crime Pays, Yo!', 'I wunder if Heaven got a ghetto'. No question.

When I get back to the real City (the Bay is forever another country) I will have passed at least ten people I don't know, all of whom will have spoken or acknowledged me in some way. Coming up The Hayes it is again as if I don't exist. Inscrutable Cardiff. Good to be back.

Mt St Sq Potted Guide

St Stephen's Church 1902 replaces temp iron church. Art space
Cambrian Buildings (site of Butetown National School)
Beynon House (orig Baltic Buildings, Atlantic Buildings, Saint Line
House) iron ore
Three-storey Houses 2nd stage house building
Empire House coal
Plain Two-Storey Georgian
Imperial House scallop windows
Aberdare House coal
Marine House scallop windows
Baltic house (orig three houses & Welsh Independent Chapel)
galleons
Coal and Shipping Exchange (Guest glassworks sticky clay nine
meters, then gardens)
Gloucester House bank
Perch town houses German consulate, Brazilian vice-consulate
Imperial House (orig Merthyr House) docks
Ship and Pilot (orig two cottages)
Mount Stuart House (orig two cottages) 1898 Cory now Academi

WINDSOR ESPLANADE GOING NORTH

Neil Sinclair brought us here. King of the Tiger Bay Walking Tours. As part of the Academi Bay Lit Festival of 1999 he'd been commissioned to walk a couple of dozen literateurs from the refurbished Norwegian Church to the unreconstructed Esplanade, taking in history and literature en-route. Not that there was much lit. Most of what we got came from Ifor Thomas who'd been commissioned to appear from behind lamp posts and out of door ways, reciting new-minted vocal verse as he came. In the organising of the event Sinclair and Thomas had not seen quite eye to eye. Sinclair insisted on wall-to-wall history – the Butes, the coal hoists, the canal, Shirley Bassey's old house. Thomas wanted at least 'I loved her a lot in Splott' and 'Smoking with Lolita'[1]. Then he wanted to do that bit where he recites poems about the Severn Bridge while doing press-ups and follows it with an imitation of Gillian Clarke in a bathrobe. They compromised. Fifty minutes of history and three poems. The last one was on the Esplanade.

Windsor Esplanade – as far south as Cardiff goes – is a Victorian terrace, twenty houses of three story bath stone directly overlooking the Bay. It's a year later now and the sun slopes in low from the west. There's a cat on top of the sea wall, someone fixing a van, a recently repainted house with a sticker reading BEWARE OF OWNER on the front window and a colour shot of Lady Di above. South, beyond the sea wall, lies the last bit of unsubmerged marsh land, sea grass and reed running a hundred metres to the water. The East Mud on the old maps. No one comes here, the Esplanade isn't on any route. If it were not for the metal strut and glass bulk of Sir Rocco Forte's St David's Hotel blocking the light from the east this could be the front at Aberystwyth or, more likely, the quieter Borth. It has that peeled lethargy reminiscent of the way the Victorians fronted their sea. I half expect to see a sign saying *B&B Rooms To Let*. This won't last, of course. Cardiff Bay waterfront is immensely valuable. At the Penarth side of the Esplanade the new Yacht Club is being built. The focus will soon shift. But it hasn't done so yet.

Beyond the far end of the Esplanade was where the Glamorgan Canal once reached Cardiff Harbour. The sea lock, the basin, the iron bridge that carried James Street over it, the notorious Old Sea Lock public house, the tenemented streets, the barges, the sounds and smells of commerce have all vanished like morning mist. All I can hear now are the cars roaring up out of the Bute Tunnel and across the Bay Bridge towards the Vale. I decide to take the long walk to town up the grassed-over old canal route. The turf is frost hard under my feet. There's a dog, a black kid with a silver scooter. Three sparrows. As I pace north the graffiti begins to thicken.

Across James Street, back of Mount Stuart Square, is the one remaining canal memory – a tow-rope bollard embedded in the tarmac, thick with spray paint, local tags, a chip in the side, no way of telling if that was done last week or two hundred years back. Beyond it, in the car park of the College of Music and Drama, a pair of students practice two-handed sword fighting, a breathless slash, clash and thrust between the Toyotas. There's no audience, not yet.

Further north the grass widens, the jetsam thickens. Two kids go past with a shopping cart full of bust furniture, settee ends, armchair backs. Someone hurls a rusted wheel barrow over a fence. Smoke smears up from distant, leafless bushes. The ancient corrugated iron fencing that separates this strip from industrial Dumballs Road to the west has more spray lettering than black bitumen. The Butetown high rises look increasingly derelict from this angle. There's been an attempt to build a new entrance porch onto one but it's unfinished, sloping back seamlessly into a debris that fills the street. This is the second Butetown. The first, the Tiger Bay that everyone remembers, was bulldozed in a fit of fifties council clearance. It was replaced with brick links, three story tenemented flats and bright towers. Streets in the skies. How the new world would be. That's what we all thought.

As I pass them now there's an air of failure. Some of the tenements have been smashed and abandoned, their windows and doors sealed with perforated metal sheet, then paint smeared and scrawled on. The gardens alternate between bright lines of kids clothing and fat stacks of mattress, carpet, broken wardrobes, pulped cardboard, and fridges with their doors gone. Occasionally someone has brightened their frontage by painting it lime green and bolting on new B&Q doors in the style of Spanish haciendas. A woman in a veil, heavy in her golden sandals, stops to rest on one of the street's backless benches. I'd like her to light up a cigarette and inhale deeply. But she won't. As I go by in my black shoes, heavy jacket and leather gloves she looks the other way. Between us is a child's bouncer on a stout industrial spring, bright red, untouched. Beyond an Astra with a wheel missing. Three men on a corner telling each other how the world is. One with an Aldi carrier. One with a folded paper. One with a stick.

This is the area John Williams covers in *Five Pubs, Two Bars and A Nightclub* and again in *Cardiff Dead*. He's from Cardiff but not from here. Locals are vaguely suspicious of what he says. There's a fly poster advertising *Dead* pasted onto the side of a BT relay box. Half ripped off. You can't get the book in the local shop, that's full of *Cardiff Yesterday* and Mills and Book romance

The grass widens to form a soccer pitch and a children's play area. The climbing frames, rope tunnels and mazes are unweathered and in use. The pitch is empty but for three youths smoking. This is the back of St Mary's where the church spirit mingles with the mosque's iron grip – less here, maybe, than it would like to be. Although no one has painted anything on its Islamic, squat brick sides. A race of kids on bikes roars passed, two clouting a can with sticks in a street version of polo. This is Canal Parade where north Butetown runs out of steam in the face of the glittering city. But the clutter of stamped can and plastic stays as thick as ever.

The Parade teeters round the back of the primary school and empties into the bright Callaghan Square, pride of the city fathers, a matter of new civic pride. The square is large, full of stone benches, fountains, trees, Barcelona lamps and evergreen plantings. To the west the vandalised art of Amber Hiscott and David Pearl's towers shines. When I reach it, a bright Saturday, the space is full of skate-boarders, forty or so, baggies, cut-shorts with heavy flap pockets, smooth-bottomed, extra-wide trainers, caps and rucksacks, and the fastest boards you can get. The new stone surfaces are criss-crossed with wheel gouges. The stone benches are clanged, whapped and jumped on by air borne boarders, skidding along their surfaces in an acrobatic rush. No one here is selling anything. The silver bike racks are empty. No one is feeding the birds. A maroon diesel engine the size of a pantechnicon tows a hundred wagons across the bridge under which the canal once passed. Old city again. But made new. Of course.

PORT

The sand stacked like sculpture along the north side of the Roath Dock won't be here for much longer. Adventurers Quay[2] encroaches. The economics of selling more pine-floored residential units vs. a few thousand tons of dredged aggregate has shifted in favour of the former. The chrome Bay moves southwards. Like a 405-line television the industrial past shrinks towards a flickering dot. At their height the docks at Cardiff occupied an area of more than 1,000 acres. What's left, now that the coal is gone and we are down to meat storage and medical supplies for the government of St Helena, is less than a third of that.

The Port itself – what remains – Queen Alexander, Roath Dock, Roath Basin – has hermetically sealed itself from the rest of the city. Its entrances are guarded by rising barriers. You don't get in without a pass. In the seventies I went through here in my Renault 9, stuffed with screaming kids, unchallenged. This splendour of French engineering had been assembled from two wrecks welded into one low-mileage, single-owner bargain and sold on to me by Dovey Motors. It broke down outside Spillers' grain mill, the vast white cathedral visible from everywhere in the city. A bunch of gangers tried to bump start me up Clipper Road. No go. The kids had to walk home while I called the garage. Couldn't happen now. The mill is bricked shut. The wharf is silent. If you are not wearing a Bob the Builder luminous yellow hard-hat and vest you can't get in.

I'm at the ABP offices with John Briggs, a soft-spoken mid-Westerner from St Paul who moved here in the 70s. He now reckons he's lived more of his life in Wales than he ever did in the States. Yet his accent hasn't altered at all. Why do I want to see the Port, I'm asked by an official. Who am I? Being a writer doesn't seem to cut it. I go down on the permit as a photographer. I take a snap of the issuing officer to confirm my credentials. She smiles.

John, the real photographer, had taken a large number of full-plate b&w shots of Butetown and the Docks when he first came to Wales. He's back now to track changes and even across thirty somewhat less than industrial years they've been immense. The steelworks has gone: the ship repair, the dry docks, the boat builders, the vast timber floats have all vanished. The polluted mud flats, home of a thousand wading birds, are now permanently under water. The bay has its snaking barrage.

There are bright signs at the Port's entrance. Paint job. Tarmac. Uniformed security. We drive in from the glass and sparkle of the waterfront architecture and step back to the Cardiff that used to be. Tip, dereliction, trails of smoke, a battered burger van, a fork lift shifting something through the corrugated doors of a nineteenth century brick warehouse, a dark truck offloading scrap, oily roadway, a diesel shunting flatbeds bearing coiled steel, a man in overalls on an ancient push bike, the water in Roath Basin shining, a few ships. On the long wharfs buried railtrack, bollards with nothing moored to them. Above

an unmoving grey sky. There's a radio playing somewhere. Macy Gray. I take a snap. John doesn't bother. I'd wanted to walk here but the place is just too large. We drive to the now abandoned Bailey's Bute Dry Dock. This is the other side of the tracks from the white re-built and re-sited Norwegian Church and its mirror steel art work (*Palisade* by Denys Short) which hides the lock machinery. There are

Americans strolling there with ice creams in their hands. Kids on skateboards. Push chairs. No one waves.

At Bailey's we're outside the Cardiff Boat Building Company founded turn of the century, leaking smoke from a yard waste fire tended by an 80 year old retired miner. Cardiff Boat made the lifeboats for the Cutty Sark, built the Scottish Island Fishery vessels, repaired just about every local sailor's dingy and rowboat, made a yacht or two for those who had the money and the desire. Now the lease is up, they're compulsorily purchased, to be swept away and the site developed as a leisure money-spinner. But for the moment, amazingly, they're still functioning. Just. Lynn and Mac, seventy year old shipwrights wielding adzes, drills and wrenches. They've got a yacht they're slowly brightening up for the owner. Mr Dovey. Didn't he once own the local Renault franchise? The very same.

In their time they'd built the *Compass Rose, the June Starfish, the Homarius, the Carlo, the Silver Puff.* Lynn shows me an oil stained notebook with its binding missing and half its pages held in with yellow-crisp sellotape. It's a hand scrawled record of everything the company has done since the works began. The first entry is 1913. On the wall are faded shots of boats and owners. The wall calendar nude, unadulterated, is for 1992. Mac tells us about the sink holes in the mud and the way the unwary would find their boats listing unusably when the tide receded. He spins tales of adventures in the channel, of tugs wrecking their charges, of ships with their keels murderously buckled by the sea rocks beyond the flats. And Shirley Bassey, she lived round here, she did. Not in Butetown but in Portmanmoor Road, Splott. Gone now. Didn't sound so good, Splott, did it? So they

has her coming from Tiger Bay. The Docks. White mother. Black father. He vanished early, sailed off. Bet he's regretted it. I used to see her in the shops. Would she recognise you, I ask? No, I was young then. Ah, but so was she. The yard radio kicks out All Saints. Lynn whacks a floor plank with the adze and smiles at the camera. John Briggs takes his shot.

On the import wharf at Queen Alexandra the *RMS St*

Helena is being loaded. A crane swings on some piping. Passengers queue, a couple of them, cases, passports too, I guess. St Helena is five thousand miles away in the south Atlantic. A distant speck of a Colony, no airstrip, ten miles long, six wide, about the size of greater Cardiff but with a population of only 5,644. Its annual ship sails from here. This is it.

Further on is the sea lock and the mud. From here, by the wrecked coastguard lookout and the disused oil storage, all butterfly bush and rust, you can see the channel side of the barrage[3]. Dumped rock, banked and compacted. Three giant black steel dolphins prevent ships from grounding. Welcome to the Port of Cardiff, it says, behind me. The deputy harbour master comes out of his hut and waves us back from the dock edge. The plastic brim of my standard-issue yellow helmet scratches my forehead. John Briggs has his on back to front. On the old maps all of this area, from Queen Road South to Longships Road and the coast path, was full of railway. A comb of shunting, sheds and tracks, places for passing, sidings where you load. Nothing now. We round the point, clamber through mud and bushes, over sea wall rock and find them. Stacked: ties, rails, sleepers. Scrap thousands. Oil. Slush. A ginger cat streaks through the long grass. Life still.

But some industry does remain. The Port is up on marine aggregates, bulk liquid, Texaco diesel, container traffic, timber, wire rod, steel bar, chill and cold store, agribulks, coke, sand, pet food and the pulp you turn into fruit juice. You get big trucks here. High sides. Artics. Trains still run. It's enough to stay open, just.

At the foot of Spillers grain mill, mothballed, the unloading conveyors slide out across the Roath Dock. Beyond, neat piles of sorted recycle glint in their pyramids. They are spaced out along the wharf – steel, alloy, aluminium. This was once Griffithmoor, edge of the sea. Now it's at least a quarter of a mile inland. Inside the fenced, reclaimed post-industrial wastes here they run the annual Network Q Rally. Fifty seriously souped GTIs engaged in a roaring spiral for money. Following the event last time South Wales Police booked 250 drivers for speeding on the public highway. Only one turned out to be an actual rally entrant. The infection of speed. We're on the edge of Splott here. Land of traffic calmers and sleeping policemen. No one roars, there isn't room.

Next time I think I'll cycle through here, I tell John. Engage with the Port landscape. Take the air. Not a good idea, he says. This place is tough on tyres and if you leave your bike to look at the water by the time you get back it could no longer be there. I look over my shoulder. There's no one in sight for miles. I think John worries too much.

The Boatbuilders' Bins

French Chalk
Hook Bolts
Wiper Motor
Nails
Brass Fittings
Bolts
Various Body Moulding Clips
Studs
Allen Keys
Air Line Fittings
Locking Tabs
Gauges
Split Pins 2" x 5/32
Large Drills
Brake Pipes
Valves
Slot drills 5/8" and 1/2"
Hose Clips
Keys
Plain Washers
illegible
Joints Universal
blank
Duchamp
crossed out

FLAT HOLM

Flat Holm – lighthouse, gulls, mist and rock. It's out there in the Bristol Channel in full view. Most Cardiffians have spent a life gazing but few have ever reached it. It's three miles in a straight line out from Lavernock point. Not far, but enough. Geographically it's the final extension of the Mendip hills that bump up through Somerset. Surprisingly it does not belong to Bristol, Avon, Barry or the Vale but is administratively a district of Cardiff County. Does the Lord Mayor know, I wonder. Does he drive across there in his Rolls? Unlikely. Flat Holm and its Cornish pastie near neighbour, Steep Holm, don't even have so much as a paved pathway between them.

Flat Holm is a mere 500 metres in diameter. It has three beaches, many rocky points and something called Dripping Cove. As its name implies, it's flat. It has none of the mystery of its steeper neighbour. The treasure or the shipwreck or the lost tribe will not be over the brow of the next hill. Stand in the centre of Flat Holm and you can see its entire world.

I come here in early September on the motor vessel *Lewis Alexander*, with thirty other visitors. The sea is as smooth as I can remember it. Flat, dull iron. No one is sick. Disembarking is a push over. There is a blackbird sitting at the top end of the jetty. Quite like home. Usually the island is the haunt of thousands of pairs of breeding gulls who feed off the rubbish tips of south Wales and fly back with their booty. The Warden keeps a collection of what comes back that's inedible – combs, hairspray bottles, bathplugs, empty Jif lemons, a joke rubber fried egg, the head of a toy dog, the leg from a doll. All carried by beak. Visitors are warned to wear a hat or hold a stick above their heads to ward off the defensive dive-bombing of the gulls. But September is not the breeding season. The birds are not at home.

Rosie, our guide from Fife, is a volunteer who's been here six months and whose accent is as impenetrable as that of someone from Llanystumdwy. She takes us from the farmhouse to the refurbished barracks and shows us the small Flat Holm museum. Here is a Neolithic axe head found during the excavation of the island's great treasure, the graves of the two murderers of Thomas à Becket. These last resting places can, of course, also be found elsewhere in Britain. But that's how it often is with the medieval world. Next to the axe head is a bulb taken from the Victorian lighthouse, a large key reputed to be from an earlier manifestation of the farmhouse (or even from the monastery that preceded it) and finally a small collection of books including Captain Marryat's sea adventures and the selected poems of Glamorgan's Professor of Poetry, Tony Curtis. Outside we discover Flat Holm's unique slow worm (it has a larger blue spot on its side than its mainland cousins), Flat Holm's unique wild peony (which also grows of Steep Holm), and Flat Holm's unique collection of wild leek (which also grow in Cornwall). These are Triffid-like and magnificent – four foot tall and with flower heads like giant rattles. At the centre of the island are the remains of a WW2 radar station. The whole of Flat Holm is littered with military left-overs. These go back through several centuries centering on the hardware generated by Palmerston's not entirely irrational fear that madman Napoleon the Third would actually invade. There are eighteenth-century cannon, earthwork emplacements and a defensive ditch which runs right across the island. This hollow is home to the marauding Alder, which is not officially classified as a tree, and the single Flat Holm horse chestnut, which is. This pathetic mid-channel example of the form, revered by Flat Homers, looks pretty stunted and lifeless to me.

At the south end Yves and I examine Bottleswell Battery and its rusting Victorian cannon, looking for where you lit the powder. Yves Gauducheau, wearing dungarees and wellington-style overshoes, is a volunteer from Nantes in France. He's a retired judge who has been coming here for years. How he explains to his wife and colleagues back home that he is devoting his free time now to a featureless, rained-on speck off the coast of south Wales I am unsure. He came at first to improve his English but since there are only ever three or four full-time residents at any one time this proved to be limiting. He could hardly spend his evenings conversing at the pub. The nearest is on Steep Holm and, there, the landlord actually travels out on the same boat as the visitors, jumping off first and nipping up the cliff to turn on the lights and set out the glasses before anyone arrives.

Yves is a bit of a *bricaleur* who can turn his hand to anything. He shows me the wall he's re-laid and, proudly, the great fog-horn engines he's re-engineered. Our guide informs us in an accent so strong it could knock down trees that Victoria was always worried about the distrustful, conniving French. Half of the military remains you see here were built to keep them away.

Flat Holm's bookshop is a cupboard in the corner of the farmhouse. It opens for twenty minutes towards the end of each visitor trip. I negotiate 50p off the price of John Barrett's *Flat Holm During World War 2* because it has a coffee stain on the back. My fellow visitors boo, believing that this is an inappropriate tactic when dealing with a charity that needs to raise a million and a half in order to refurbish their miserably out-of-condition Grade Two Listed Cholera Isolation Hospital. Outside is the little metal flash that forms the Guglielmo Marconi memorial. The first radio signal arrived in May 1897, transmitted by Marconi crouched among the ferns on Lavernock Point. ARE YOU READY, it read. You can see why he chose this island. To celebrate the fact I call home on my Orange mobile. We're leaving now, I say. Unlike many places in Wales the signal here is perfect.

NEWTOWN

Can a whole district – houses, people, even the name – simply disappear? They can. Ask your average Cardiffian if they know where Newtown is and they'll tell you it's in mid-Wales. Of the vanished local little Ireland they know nothing at all. I'd first heard of the slum-cleared Newtown by following a link from Barry Tobin's Welsh-Irish website. Barry, a former librarian, multi-linguist and expert on the Irish Famine, has more local Irish links running off his html creation than Dublin has bars. Scrape the Cardiff surface and you'll find shamrocks underneath.

Newtown was built by Bute in 1846 to house Irish workers fleeing the potato famine by sailing from Cork as human ballast on the coal ships that plied industrial trade across St George's Channel. During Cardiff's boom there was a vast need for labour. Docks were to be worked, railways laid, buildings to be slung up, pig iron to be loaded. The district consisted of six streets – Pendoylan Street, Roland Street, North William Street, Rosemary Street, Pendoylan Place and Ellen Street – two hundred houses – jammed, insanitarily, back-to-back, in the sliver of ground between the main rail line and Tyndall Street. A warren of bedrooms used in relays above cramped,

over-occupied parlours and damp, unventilated kitchens were home
to more than a thousand immigrants. There were shops, pubs (five in
one street alone in the early years) and two churches – the Roman
Catholic St Pauls's which was always full and dominated local life
almost as much as the drink did, and the Welsh All Saints which
scratched a congregation from somewhere, just. There was smoke
and unsurfaced streets, steam and roofs which leaked, the roar of the
steel works and the clank and clatter of trains. Newtown was never
silent. You could hear your neighbour breathing. There were tiny back
yards made from uneven flag and rough grass. There were no trees.
Not one.

Newtown wasn't the only Irish area of Cardiff – the Hayes, and the
cramped courts and back streets around Bridge and Mary Ann
Streets were almost uniformly green – but Newtown was an island.
Bounded by the rail line to the north, the goods yard to the east,
feeder to the west, and the dock itself to the south it developed a
particularly strong sense of community.

Mary Sullivan, who runs the present day Newtown Association, a
sort of virtual Cardiff Irish community of the web, was born in
Newtown and is the centre of many commendable attempts to keep
the name alive. Her grandmother shovelled potatoes for Edward
England from boats wharfed at the top of West Bute, three hundred
yards from Ellen Street. England's warehouse is still there, stranded,
the filled-in West Bute now a manicured park, the factories around it
turned to offices or glass apartment. We meet in the forecourt. I'm
carrying a newspaper so she can recognise me. *The Western Mail*,
news of the Irish troubles still on page one. She leaves her car where

the wharf edge once was, next
to a berberis bush, planted for
the enjoyment of new residents
at the nearby Lloyd George
apartments. Money talks.
Newtown never had any.

We cross Tyndall Street, full
of traffic, past the Willis
Corroon Group building and
the site for the proposed
Newtown Memorial Garden.
Mary is proud of this, Tarmac
have donated the land, Sir
Geoffrey Inkin and the old

CBDC have put up some development cash, artist David Mackie has planned the layout, all that's needed is the lottery money to build. Do it soon, I urge, before the developers use the space for something else. The area once filled by Newtown is now Atlantic House, the Peacock Group headquarters high rise. Doug Corker's 1991 art work, looking a lot like an oversize car badge, is to its front. This

has next to it the Tyndall Street Industrial Estate – stores, small workshops, the premises of greetings card agents, Rock Bottom Wholesale, Nature's Table Wholefoods, Fireworks & Diecast Collectables. This is inner city commerce. Round the back will be dumpsters full of cardboard waste. Inside, denim-clad truck loaders drinking tea. The name of Newtown is utterly invisible. We walk in strong sun, Mary pointing out the sites of the old pubs – the Crichton Arms, Tobins, the Cambridge, the Duke of Edinburgh, where the corner shop was, the single telephone box. Ellen Street is still there, leading to the Driscoll Workshops, named after Newtown's most famous son. In the early years of the twentieth century Peerless Jim Driscoll was Featherweight Champion of the World. When he died in 1925, 100,000 people lined the streets to watch his funeral cortège go by. The statue the city has erected to his memory is elsewhere, at the top of Bute Street. Ellen Street where he lived and died, has the Workshops – King Oak Network Installers, Brolec Contractors, Motor Tint Door and Window Maintenance.

Going back down Ellen Street a week later to check out the occupants of some of the units I spot a bloke in jeans fixing a Rover 414sli on the pavement outside an electrical wholesalers. He's got half the engine out and a whole passenger door lying on the pavement. It's amazing what you can manage to mend in your lunch break. I ask him if he knows about Newtown. Newtown, mate, nah, not round here. Never heard of it. He's changing spanners and pulling furiously at some engine part which won't budge. What about Jim Driscoll? Yeah, know him. He was a boxer, right? Back in the twenties. We knew how to do things then.

By the time Newtown was marked for demolition in 1966 it had 169 falling-down houses, two pubs and a garage. Half its population called themselves Welsh rather than Irish, but their names – O'Sullivan, O'Leary, Burns, O'Shanahan, Dwyer – gave away their origins. A proposal that the district should be rebuilt where it stood was unaccountably defeated. Families were dispersed to Ely, Pentrebane, Trowbridge and Llanrumney. The community was broken. In 1970 St Pauls, the church, the school and the presbytery, was pulled down in order to make space for the Central Link Road flyover, the route from the changing city to the redeveloping bay.

All that's left today are the fourteen standard-pattern council houses built late on the bobtail, waste ground once fronting Tyndall Street. This was a red-light district for a time after the prostitutes were moved up off the newly cleansed Bute Street. They are west of here today, near the Central Station. I ask someone mowing their front lawn if she'd heard about little Ireland. Yes, she had. Mrs Kitchen next door was here when the houses still stood. So what's the area called today? What do you put down when you write your address? Atlantic Wharf, she replies without a flicker. The mower roars.

GRANGEMORE PARC

You can feel it. At Powerhouse the day is unbelievably exciting. In this domestic electronics wonderland there are thirty-four varieties of kettle. Sell me one, I demand. The assistant is neat and keen. This model, she says, the Morphy Richards 43512/2, has high speed boil. It's blue. And this one? This model, the Kenwood Millennium, has fast boil. It's yellow. Is there a difference in the boil speeds between fast and high? No. Don't know. I can check. This one? This model, the Swan 5678H, has an autocutout. It's silver. Is it fast? Yes. No. I'll check. Is it in stock? Don't know. She goes to look. It is. You're in luck. We've Red, Black, Ocean Green, Vermilion, Pastel Bright Skyglow, Powder White, Burger Black. Azure, Speckled Gleam, Golden Sheen, Golden Lights. And Brown.

At the checkout I buy a trailing socket and a set of bags for the vacuum cleaner. Everyone pays either cash or extended credit. In front a mother and daughter strung with twins, babyfeeders and a shopping bag on wheels pay £445 in fivers for a teletext-able widescreen. The lad'll put it in the taxi for you. The cashier doesn't ask if they want that. He knows. His hair is slicked down like he's just stepped from the shower. He smiles at everyone. Exuding joy. Yes, next, love, thank you. £230 in tenners for an imitation Dyson. In front of me a late fifties, track suit bottoms, trainers, battered by fags, signs up for monthly payments on a camcorder and new edit-function four-head Nicam Stereo. The deal is over in about ninety seconds. Form, status check, signature. Yes, good, they'll contact you. Smile. Next. Thank you.

This is the Cardiff Bay Retail Park, south of Grangetown, built where Ferry Road and its car dismantlers ran into the sink and salt marsh of Penarth Moors. The lights of Asda play strong across the huge car park, its bays, walkways, evergreen plantings and street art. There's an assemblage outside Powerhouse which looks like a tree made of the sails of ships. In the late afternoon the low sun winks off its furls. Black kids go past on shining scooters. No one looks up.

Beyond a low green hill surmounted by what, at this distance, looks like a hill fort. This used to be the south Cardiff landfill – the squall of circling seabirds, the rush and drone of trucks, the dump. Now it's been topped with hardcore, soil, planted, walled, drained, landscaped. CBDC have regenerated this as Grangemore Parc, "a refuge from the city." That's what it says on the notice board at the entrance. You go in over a stile and it feels for all the world like the wild moors of the Brecon Beacons – rough tracks, stone walls, surface water, a destination and a climb to the top. The fort is an art work. Ian Randell's *Silent Links*, a contruct of stone and ship's anchor chains. They couple themselves into the hill top, huge and somnolent. A few are broken open, half buried. The past comes undone.

I walk about and get my town shoes thoroughly muddy. The paths slide and bend as they might at Cadbury Castle. It's hard to reconcile the wet wildness with the proximity of the Grangetown gasholders, the Butetown Link road below and the barrage in the distance. To the north I can see the Millennium Stadium and the shining city. I'm a refugee. Nobody else is. There are picnic tables at the car park fringes, tidy, unvandalised, replete with bins on posts, shrub plantings, water features. There's a Welsh Pennant dry-stone wall from Gelligaer (bi-lingual history and background interpretation board – Jo Johnson, Landscape Architects. Call 02920 873333 for more information). And me, walking. A notice sellotaped to a fingerpost offers a reward for the return of a lost black cat. There are gulls.

Through the gate, back in the car park, the shoppers are laughing. You can spend your life here filling the boot with stuffed bags and bright boxes. If the spirit flags Macdonalds will blandly revive it. I wipe the mud from the sides of my shoes on the grass verge. Two Japanese head for Boots. Someone has bought a white ash table and is strapping it to his roof rack. The litter is all in its bins. Behind me, outglittered and invisible, the refuge stands empty. Except for a dark cat, sliding through the long grass, and a solitary Asda carrier flapping on the fence.

A WEST BUTE DOCK WALK

The Marquis's great Bute West Dock, opened in 1839. Its first ship was the *Manulus* from Quebec. As a mineral exporter Cardiff had a head start on the rest of south Wales and for a time, as things turned, the rest of the world. At nineteen and a half acres in size the Bute West was soon outgrown. Docks blossomed, to the east, to the south. The Bute West hung on loading coal, importing timber, shipping iron rails to the whole world. But in 1964, faced with maritime decline and the end of the coal industry, it was filled in.

The walk, the only formal one in this book, should take around an hour. Park at the north end of where this west Dock once was, opposite the rough tarmaced lot of Edward England Potato Merchant's storefront. This is Tyndall Street. Parking here is safe enough, but put bags in the boot and apply the steering lock.

The walk goes down the east side of the original West Bute Dock Feeder which glides its dark water – currently full of trash and discoloured traffic cones – between a new office development and the potato merchant's last outpost. The Feeder is as wide as a canal here, although it never carried boats. The top edge of the West Dock is now a concrete kerb, all that's left, facing the top end of a new park and the Lloyd George Avenue housing development. The Feeder, negotiating an overflow pump, bears left, bound for the entrapped East Bute, redeveloped as a leisure pool for fishermen, powerboats and Chinese

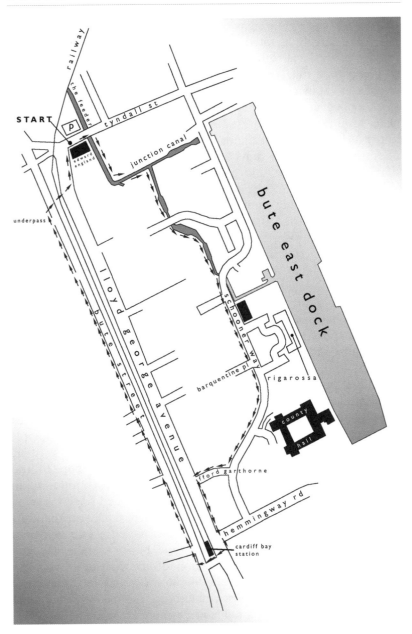

a west bute dock walk

dragon boat races. The signs warn against green algae and infection. They are largely ignored as a perfunctory legislative obligation fulfilled by the local authority in advance of possible litigious attack.

The path, a full, paved walkway, moves through late 90s professional-class housing, pillared entrances, double-glazed porchways, a clock incongruously on the eves, neo-Georgian confections, no two alike, brought here from Boston or from Mars. The water crawls under its bridges, round angular turns, making this a Cardiff version of Amsterdam. Take a right turn to pass through the centre of the development. Willows and garden plantings banish any notion of industrialisation. Ducks. Cats. A swan.

The path, a steady eight minute stroll, eventually emerges to the right of The Wharf, a Brains leisure pub that exists on quiz nights, live music, cheap sizzle steak and Dylan's Ale. You can sit outside here and gaze across the East Bute water at the one remaining dock crane and imagine that you are in a slicker metropolis. But the shrieks of crisp eating children soon bring you back to Welsher earth.

Continue south along Schooner Way, past the cod Italian Rigarossa housing development (Club Med with drizzle) and the seafaring new streets – Hilliard Court, Corvette Court, and Barquentine Place. On your left is the pagoda roofed South Glamorgan, now Cardiff, County Hall. The landscaped car park is full of Fiat Brava, Ford Focus and shining Ford Fiestas on three-year lease purchase.

Schooner Way points straight at the north end of the UCI complex multi-screen, restaurants, echoing bowling alley, night club, multiple cash dispensers pouting their essential mouths at the arriving throngs. Before you reach it cut right through the short Ffordd Garthorne onto Lloyd George Avenue. Turning left continue south along this brand new, multi-traffic light embellished boulevard that connects the old city with the new. The area here is dense with industrial dock memorabilia fixed onto pavement edge like works of sculptural art. Crane hooks, chains, hoists, buckets, grabs, anchors. Poor recompense for the destruction of the Maritime Museum which was demolished in the late 90s to make way for a bunch of new-build bars and minimalist restaurants. The exhibits that could be moved were stored in a rail siding near Treforest. The big stuff, including the magnificent tug *The Sea Alarm*, were surreptitiously cut up and sold as scrap.

At the traffic lights, with the red brick Pier Head Building (now the National Assembly's public information and interpretation point) directly ahead and the new Wales Millenium Centre to its left, take a right. Note the three story chrome art work and fountain as focus to the Lloyd George boulevard. The station-like building on your right is just that – the former Bute Road terminus, still serving time as Cardiff Bay station, unmanned, but recipient of a regular, if over-priced,

train service back up to Cardiff's Queen Street. The station here was once to be the home of the local railway preservation society and, for a time, had toy trains on show within and real preserved steam locos in the sidings outside. But, like the sidings themselves, they vanished under Bay regeneration.

Just beyond the butt end of the railway lies Bute Street, the traffic calmed, edge planted, resurfaced and rekerbed original main thoroughfare to Cardiff Docks. It's clean, over-tidy, little graffitied and only a pale shadow of what it once was. Take a steady walk north, past Brandon Tool Hire, the Loudon Square shops, the church of St Mary and St Stephen, and the Letton underpass on the right which takes foot traffic under the rail link and back to the Mediterranean housing development which runs along the east side of Lloyd George.

The pavements here are free of docks-era industrial memorabilia but not of new public art. The normally sensitive Cardiff Bay Arts Trust, responsible for such brilliant additions to the Cardiff street environment as Sally Matthews' *Drift of Curlews* near St David's Hotel and Pierre Vivant's *Landmark 1992* assemblage of traffic signs adorning the Windsor Road traffic island at the entrance to Splott, have installed ten gleaming street pillars to celebrate former Bute Street buildings – the Cairo Hotel, the Powell Duffryn Steam Coal Co., and more. They are accompanied by a raft of embossed and engraved pavers: kids drawings, South African shillings, bits of poetry, Islamic zig zag, fish, memorials to one-armed Joe Erskin, to Shirley Bassey, to the things that happened here. There's no doubting the quality, nor the innovation, it's the density that seems at fault.

Small price, however. At least it *is* art.

At the top end, as Bute Street approaches Callaghan Square. Take a right through the rail line underpass. You'll emerge at the north end of Lloyd George Avenue facing, once again, Edward England's potato warehouse. There's the car park and your car. No one has taken it. No one has broken in. There are no scratch marks along its side. Check the sky. Any sun? No. This is Cardiff. Expect drizzle. When it's dry that's a bonus.

BACK TO THE BAY

I'm on the Central Link road heading back to the Bay. Below me is the main rail line to London and in front the straight sweep past the sanitised East Dock. Capitol Waterfront is ahead. New rise, brick and glass, angular roofs made to resemble ship decks or waves, human scale, no sky scraping. You are not allowed to walk or cycle this road, there's a sign, not that this stops anyone. The Mercs and BMWs heading for Adventurers Quay slide past a guy in builders' boots on a black Raleigh and a woman in black robes towing a shopping cart. The double roundabout, centred with decorative quarried stones and multi-coloured bark mulch, spills us around Nippon Electric Glass and sends us to the pagoda structures of County Hall, the Bute Tunnel west or on to the waterfront centre of power. This is the renamed Crickhowell House, the Cynulliad Genedlaethol, the National Assembly. Across what used to be Britannia Road is the space Richard Rogers' controversial National Assembly Debating

Chamber is going in. Funnel roofs, glass, access, visible government, a cascade of steps to the waterside, removed because the disabled couldn't handle them, amended, restored for the sake of art and balance. Still not built as I write. But starting soon.

The Assembly is in Cardiff because it couldn't be anywhere else. The long pseudo-debate surrounding its site lead authorities in Wrexham, Dolgellau and

Swansea into believing they had a case. People got excited. Reports were written and municipal hopes encouraged. Nothing came of them, naturally. How can a government be situated anywhere but in its country's capital? But behind this easy answer lies a suspicion. Most of the Welsh south east who bothered to vote declared that they wanted no part in any kind of devolved parliament.

Glamorgan County Council on stilts, the Cardiff *South Wales Echo* called it. Did Cardiff really want it? But build the new Assembly in Machynlleth and it would treated as a distant joke. The moment for unity would be lost. The Assembly went to the Bay, a magnet among the silver minimalism, the signs saying *Crickhowell House* vanished. Britannia Road became Pier Head Street.

At *Art at the Assembly,* a series of sponsorship-generating performances mounted in the Assembly's milling area lunch-times before formal sessions, we eat canapés and strawberries dipped in chocolate. There's wine. The suits glide. The First Secretary is there, he's introduced the performance. The Minister talks business to arts activists. There's a scattering of AMs and a collection of selected arts users. The show is fifteen minutes from Theatr Iolo, Kevin Lewis in baggy trousers doing a mid-European accented piece of thespian brilliance designed to cross age frontiers and impress the hell out of the assembled worthies. It does.

Outside, where street sculpture and architectural detailing meet in a Disneyesque melée locals wonder when the largesse is going to reach them. Mount Stuart Primary School has been rebuilt and a couple of service jobs have been filled by black faces at Harry Ramsden's and St David's Hotel. The Cynulliad remains largely a white reservation. Demographically correct for Wales but a bit odd down here.

I walk out along the waterfront. Wooden-decked, art encrusted, moving ever so close to the unfortunate border with down-market tat. The Pearl of the Orient has a white jacketed pianist sitting at a grand just inside their window. Someone is handing out free samples of juiced mango in an attempt to drum up custom. The tourists sup and smile. I sit at one of the outside tables at Via Fossa, a Mediterranean food emporium with a downstairs full of shine and stuffed sofas. I am asked to give them my credit card before they'll even show me a menu. It's not that we don't trust you, sir, says the waitress, staring into the middle distance, but lots of our customers run off without paying. The area's reputation is building. Or rather going back to what it once was. The Bay Art Trust have installed the complete text of John Masefield's evocative poem, *Cargoes*, on a steel slab right next to the steps that take you down to the Bay water taxi (every thirty minutes to Penarth). It's large, heavily rusting, and already splashed with cigarette ends and ice-cream daubs. The poem, about the nineteenth century dock trade, is based on Masefield's voyage to the Cape aboard a White Star Line iron barque which sailed from Cardiff in 1894.

Going back to the car along the new streets and recent refurbishments it's obvious that maintenance is a prime Cardiff difficulty. This whole south city regeneration, child of the unloved but now strangely missed CBDC, has fallen back to control by the council. And, despite setting up something called the *Inner Harbour Authority*, they do not handle maintenance well. Litter levels are up, graffiti stays, rust is not painted over. In the Butetown streets debris remains where it's been dumped. Break things and they seem to stay broken. Do we lack pride? I don't think so. We just appear unable to turn the right bureaucratic switch. The sweepers stay in Queen Street. Litter pickers work the City Hall lawns. The contracted-out repair gangs are all employed on the forecourt of the Hilton Hotel.

Is that it? Cardiff, a place that when it breaks doesn't get fixed? As I write I hear that St David's Hotel have complained. The accumulated trash is not good for trade. Teams of workers have been seen pulling weeds out of boulevard plantings. Floating polystyrene cups have been fished out of water features. Money, once again, does the talking.

notes

1. 'I Loved Her A Lot In Splott' and 'Smoking With Lolita' are both classic Ifor Thomas performance poems. The texts are in Thomas's selected poems, *Unprotected Sex*, published by Parthian Books.

2. Adventurers Quay is not simply an empty name invented by marketeers selling square footage to monoglot executives. In 1910 Scott sailed to the Antarctic from here in *Terra Nova*.

3. The Cardiff Bay Barrage, jewel of the Development Corporation's crown, its greatest and most hotly disputed legacy, holds back the waters of the Taf and the Ely, turning their collective mouths into a vast fresh water lagoon. 200 hectares. Boating, watersports. Shimmering skylines. They've spent £14m diverting sewage outfalls and cleansing the water. No floaters. No oil rainbows. But I wouldn't swim here. I looked the other week and, amazingly, I could see rocks below, unobscured by grey darkness. Canton has yet to find its cellars full of groundwater. The haze of mosquito has not yet arrived. Money has been spent to keep them away. But there's time. Path and parks along the barrage top are not complete. You cannot yet walk from Queen Alexander to Penarth Head. Is the £200m wonder a success? Are the wading birds happier in the mud along the Gwent Levels? Jury's still out.

APPENDIX 1: THE PHOTOGRAPHS

All photographs by Peter Finch, apart from p29, Daniel Finch.

APPENDIX 2: WORKS CONSULTED

Alexandrian, Sarane, *Surrealist Art*, Thames & Hudson, 1970

Allen, S.W., *Reminiscences*, Cardiff, 1918

Amgueddfa Werin Cymru, *Museum of Welsh Life Visitor Guide*, National Museum of Wales, 1998

Andrews, Steve, *Herbs of the Northern Shaman*, Loompanics Unlimited, 2000

Barrett, John, *Flat Holm During World War 2*, John Barrett, 1992

Barton, Nicholas, *The Lost Rivers Of London*, Historical Publications, 1982

Betts, Clive, *Cardiff & The Eisteddfod*, Gwasg ap Dafydd, 1978

Billingham, Nigel & Stephen K. Jones, *Images of Wales – Ely, Caerau and Michaelston-Super-Ely*
        Tempus, 1996

Billingham, Nigel & Stephen K. Jones, *Images of Wales – Ely Common To Culverhouse Cross*, Tempus, 1999

Briggs, John, *Before The Deluge*, Seren, 2002

Burns, Peggy, *Memories of Cardiff*, True North Books, 1999

Cardiff County Council, *Cardiff Unitary Development Plan (1996-2016) Outline Proposals for Consultation*, Cardiff County Council, 2001

CBAT, *Decade – 10 Years of Art and Regeneration, Cardiff Bay Arts Trust 1990-2000*, CBAT, 2001.

CBDC, *Renaissance – The Story of Cardiff Bay 1987-2000*, CBDC, 2000

Chappell, Edgar L., *History of the Port of Cardiff*, Priory Press, 1939

Chappell, Edgar L., *Old Whitchurch – The Story of a Glamorgan Parish*, The Priory Press, 1945

Childs, Jeff, *Images of Wales – Roath, Splott and Adamsdown*, Tempus, 1995

Corbett, James Andrew (editor), *A Booke of Glamorganshire Antiquities*, Rice Merrick Esq., 1578,
        Dryden Press, 1887

Davies, Dr Chrystal, *A Walk Around Llandaf Cathedral*, RJL Smith & Associates, 1999

Davies, Janet, *The Welsh Language*, University of Wales Press, 1993

Davies, John, *Studies In Welsh History, Cardiff and the Marquesses of Bute*, University of Wales Press, 1981

Day, Lance, *Broad Gauge*, Science Museum, HMSO, 1985

Fanthorpe, Lionel, *Earth, Sea and Sky – The Collected Poems of Lionel Fanthorpe*, Lionel and Patricia
        Fanthorpe, 2000

Fanthorpe, Lionel & Fanthorpe, Patricia, *The World's Most Mysterious People*, Hounslow Press, 1998

Fanthorpe, Lionel & Fanthorpe, Patricia, *The World's Most Mysterious Places*, Hounslow Press, 1999

Gillham, Mary E., *The Garth Countryside, part of Cardiff's Green Mantle*, Lazy Cat Publishing, 1999

Greenslade, David, *Cambrian Country, Welsh Emblems*, Gwasg Carreg Gwalch, 2000

Gregory, Donald, *Wales before 1066 – A Guide*, Gwasg Carreg Gwalch, 1989

Gregory, Donald, *Wales before 1536 – A Guide*, Gwasg Carreg Gwalch, 1993

Hammond, Martin, *Bricks and Brickmaking*, Shire Album No 75, Shire Publications 1981

Hannan, Patrick, *Wales Off Message – From Clapham Common to Cardiff Bay*, Seren, 2000

Hilling, John, *Plans & Prospects – Architecture in Wales 1780-1914*, Welsh Arts Council, 1975

Hindess, Gordon, *Family Walks Around Cardiff and the Valleys*, Scarthin Books, 1992

Howell, Raymond, *A History of Gwent*, Gomer, 1988

Hutchinson, Robert, *Three Arts Centres – A Study of South Hill Park, the Gardner Centre and Chapter*,
        Arts Council of Great Britain, 1977

Hutton, John, *Taf Vale Railway Miscellany*, OPC 1988

Jenkins, Nigel, *Footsore On The Frontier Selected Essays and Articles*, Gomer, 2001

Jones, Barbara, *The Archive Photographs Series, Grangetown*, Chalfont, 1996

Jones, Bryan, *The Archive Photographs Series, Canton*, Tempus, 1995

Jones, Dan, *Cardiff City Observatory Handbook*, City of Cardiff Education Committee, 1931

Jones, David & Rivers, Tony, *Soul Crew, The Inside Story of Britain's Most Notorious Hooligan Gang*,
        Milo Books, 2002

Jones, Francis, *The Holy Wells Of Wales*, University of Wales Press, 1954

Jordan, Glenn, *Bert Hardy: Down The Bay*, Butetown History & Arts, 2001
Jory, Bob & Friends, *Flat Holm Bristol Channel Island*, Wincanton Press, 1995.
Llanishen History Society, *The Nant Fawr Woodlands, a community treasure*, Friends of Nant Fawr
    Community Woodlands, 2001
Lee, Brian & others, *A Cardiff Notebook*, Historic records Project, Cardiff City Council, 1988.
Lee, Brian, *Images of Wales – Cardiff Remembered*, Tempus, 1997
Lee, Brian & Butetown History and Arts Centre, *Images of Wales – Butetown and Cardiff Docks*,
    Tempus, 1999
Llandaf Society, *The Archive Photographs Series – Llandaf*, Tempus, 1996
Malkin, Benjamin Heath, *The Scenery, Antiquities and Biography of South Wales from Materials
    Collected During Two Excursions in the Year 1803*, T. N. Longman, 1804
Marsden, Hilary, *Whitaker's Almanack* (various editions), The Stationery Office
Matthews, John Hobson, *Cardiff Records, Being Materials For A History Of The County Borough From
    The Earliest Times* (six vols), 1898, 1911
Millennium Stadium, *Building For A Rugby Nation, The Official Souvenir Handbook*, Elf Media
    Group/Westgate Sports Agency, 2000
Morgan, Dennis, *Cardiff – A City at War*, Dennis Morgan, 1998
Morgan, Dennis, *Discovering Cardiff's Past*, D. Brown and Sons Ltd, 1995
Morgan, Dennis, *The Cardiff Story*, D Brown and Sons Ltd, 1991
Morgan, Rhodri, *Cardiff: Half-and-half a Capital*. Changing Wales Series, Gomer, 1994
O'Gorman, Connie & Bryant, Jo, *The Shadow of the Steelworks iii – Pengam Farm (Later Tremorfa)
    and Surroundings*, Willows Word Wizards, 1998.
O'Neill, Dan, *Tiger Bay And The Docks, The Story of a Remarkable Corner of the World*, Breedon
    Books & the South Wales Echo, 2001
Rees, William, *Cardiff – A History of the City*, The Corporation of the City of Cardiff, 1969
Sinclair, Neil M.C., *The Tiger Bay Story*, Dragon & Tiger Enterprises, 1997
Stone, C.J., *The Last of the Hippies*, Faber & Faber, 1999
Thomas, Harley (editor), *Taf Trails – Short Walks In the Taf Valley*, The Taf Trail Project, 1990
Unwin, Liz, *Discover Cardiff – Five Historical Walks Around The City*, Cardiff Marketing Ltd, 1995
Vinter, Jeff, *The Taf Trail – Official Guidebook*, Alan Sutton, 1993
Webb, Harri, *Looking Up England's Arsehole*, Y Lolfa, 2000
Whittle, Elisabeth, *A Guide To Ancient and Historic Wales – Glamorgan and Gwent*, CADW, HMSO,
    1992
Wiliam, Eurwyn, *St Fagans Castle and its Inhabitants*, National Museum of Wales, 1988
Williams, Gareth, *Life On The Heath*, Merton Priory Press, 2001
Williams, Herbert, *Railways In Wales*, Christopher Davies, 1981
Williams, Stewart (editor), *The Cardiff Book, Vols 1-3,* Stewart Williams, 1973

INDEX

THE AUTHOR

Peter Finch is a poet and literary entrepreneur who was born in Cardiff and still lives here. His lifetime output of poetry titles includes *Useful, Poems for Ghosts* and *Food* from Seren, *Antibodies* from Stride and *The Welsh Poems* from Shearsman. Seren published his *Selected Later Poems* in 2008 and will bring out *Zen Cymru* in 2010. He has written and published short fiction, criticism and a number of books on the business of writing including *How To Publish Yourself* (Allison & Busby) and *The Poetry Business* (Seren). His extensive web site is at www.peterfinch.co.uk

A former publisher and bookseller he is currently runs Academi, the Welsh National Literature Promotion Agency and Society of Writers. www.academi.org

Real Cardiff and *Real Cardiff Two* have both been Seren bestsellers and are joined in 2009 by *Real Cardiff Three*, subtitled 'The Changing City'. Peter Finch is the editor of Seren's Real series which includes volumes on the conurbations of Llanelli, Merthyr Tydfil, Wrexham, Liverpool, Aberystwyth, Swansea and Newport. His is also the author of *Real Wales*. With Grahame Davies he has compiled *The Big Book of Cardiff*, an anthology of poetry and prose which concentrates on the revitalised city.

THE CRITICS ON REAL CARDIFF

This is a marvellous book – one of the very best books about a city I have ever read. It makes me feel terribly old-fashioned – superficial too, because I have never actually lived in the cities I have written about. I skip most of the poems, which I don't understand, but everything else in it is gripping me so fast that I have momentarily suspended my first ever reading of *Wuthering Heights*.

Jan Morris

Native Cardiffians now have the definitive guide to their city... the excitement of being one of the newest European capitals hangs light in the air.

Kate Nicholson
Writers' News

A wealth of information on the significance of familiar sites for those who live in Cardiff and an interesting insight into Wales' capital for those who don't, *Real Cardiff* is far more indicative of life in the city than the average tourist guide.

Cathryn Scott
The Big Issue

Every district is covered and there is something new to discover in every section. This will be a best seller and will be the top gift on my Christmas present list this year!

Bill Barrett
Cardiff Post

The travel section of the *Observer* highlights Wales as a 'place to visit' in 2003. If you are persuaded, and would like a genuine flavour of the capital, read Peter Finch, who has studied the city in historical depth and quartered it on foot and will entertain you all the way.

Sam Adams
PN Review

The book's great strength is not in the macro but in the micro, in the deep, prolonged engagement with a particular place which has produced a richly nuanced, affectionate and sometimes exasperated portrait of a city. The beauty lies in the detail.

Grahame Davies
New Welsh Review

Cunningly intermeshed with this cornucopia of useful and fascinating material is an account of how a young man who was something or other in the City Hall became an editor, a publisher, a bookseller, an arts administrator and a poet – the most surreally inventive and provocative writer we have – without leaving the city's limits.

Meic Stephens
Cambria

This book should be read by anyone who wants to get to know more about Cardiff. That should include most people in Wales for a start. Even the ones in places like Swansea, Aberystwyth and Caernarfon.

Raymond Humphreys
Cambrensis

Lurking behind much of the text is a reassurance from Peter Finch to the reader, and from Peter Finch to himself, that the poet's place is that of an outsider, even when the poet in question has become, ostensibly at least, part of the Establishment. And that's why the subject matter fits so well. Cardiff, that deeply self-conscious and not-very-Welsh capital of Wales, that country with more chips than Barry island, is truly the outsider's metropolis.

Mike Parker
Planet

MORE VOLUMES IN THE REAL SERIES

Available at www.serenbooks.com